北部湾大学高层次人才科研启动经费项目"心理困境儿童的社会情感学习能力提升实证研究"
2022年广西教育科学规划高等教育国际化专项课题重点课题"员工关怀视角下中外合作办学机构EAP服务
2022年广西高校大学生思想政治教育理论与实践研究课题"高校心理健康教育工作的FEAP服务
2022年度北部湾大学东密歇根联合工程学院"中外合作办学教改项目中外合作办学机构员工福利与支持项目EAP服
2023年广西区级大学生创新创业训练计划立项项目"地方高校国际化和城市国际化进程中的外籍人士人文关怀服务

青少年社会情感
能力提升研究

邬德利
【著】

A Study on the
Improvement of Adolescents' Social and
Emotional Learning Abilities

四川大学出版社
SICHUAN UNIVERSITY PRESS

图书在版编目（CIP）数据

青少年社会情感能力提升研究：英文 / 邬德利著
. — 成都：四川大学出版社，2024.6
ISBN 978-7-5690-6915-0

Ⅰ. ①青… Ⅱ. ①邬… Ⅲ. ①青少年教育－情感教育
－研究－英文 Ⅳ. ① G44

中国国家版本馆 CIP 数据核字（2024）第 107388 号

书　　名：青少年社会情感能力提升研究
　　　　　Qingshaonian Shehui Qinggan Nengli Tisheng Yanjiu
著　　者：邬德利

选题策划：孙明丽
责任编辑：孙明丽
责任校对：吴连英
装帧设计：墨创文化
责任印制：王　炜

出版发行：四川大学出版社有限责任公司
　　　　　地址：成都市一环路南一段 24 号（610065）
　　　　　电话：（028）85408311（发行部）、85400276（总编室）
　　　　　电子邮箱：scupress@vip.163.com
　　　　　网址：https://press.scu.edu.cn
印前制作：四川胜翔数码印务设计有限公司
印刷装订：成都市新都华兴印务有限公司

成品尺寸：170 mm×240 mm
印　　张：13.25
字　　数：323 千字

版　　次：2024 年 6 月　第 1 版
印　　次：2024 年 6 月　第 1 次印刷
定　　价：68.00 元

扫码获取数字资源

四川大学出版社
微信公众号

Preface

    Adolescence is a crucial period for adolescents' growth, which plays a crucial role in shaping their personality and adapting to society. Due to rapid physiological changes, teenagers are in a period of rapid emotional development, and adolescents are prone to significant emotional fluctuations. The rapid changes in physiology and insufficient social cognition lead to psychological discomfort to adolescents. Meanwhile, the pressure of China's college entrance examination has led young students to prioritize their studies and have few opportunities to deeply participate in social life, which is not conducive to the cultivation of their social adaptability. At present, the detection rate of psychological problems among Chinese adolescents has significantly increased, therefore, it is urgent to improve the mental health level of students. Cognitive emotional therapy is a simple and effective psychological method that can help adolescents learn to improve their behaviors by enhancing their cognition, changing their emotions, and promoting their social adaptation and mental health.

    Social and Emotional Learning is an educational program initiated by a non-profit organization (Collaboration for Academic, Social and Emotional Learning) aimed at enhancing the social emotional abilities of adolescents. The Ministry of Education of China has collaborated with The United Nations Children's Fund to carry out a Social and Emotional Learning program to improve Chinese adolescents' social-emotional abilities. There are five SEL abilities in this programme, including recognizing and handling one's own emotions, improving care and concern for others, establishing positive relationships with others, making responsible decisions, and the last one is responding and handling challenging emergencies in a constructive and ethical manner. This book is based on the

American SEL programme "Strong kids". Through research on Chinese teenagers and combining with the characteristics of Chinese culture, it creatively developed a SEL programme suitable for Chinese teenagers and promotes its application among Chinese teenagers. Practice has shown that this program can effectively enhance social and emotional abilities of Chinese adolescents, reduce their learning anxiety, and enhance their adaptability to school. It is worth further promotion and use. The research outcome of this book won the Best Paper Award at the 14th MAPIM-KPT Malaysia in 2023. This book is suitable for educational psychology researchers, teachers, parents, adolescent students, educational administrators, and those who are interested in psychology.

I would like to express my sincere gratitude to Professor Rosna and Dr. Amrita from Universiti Utara Malaysia for their careful guidance in this research. I would also like to express my sincere gratitude to the psychology colleagues who actively supported and assisted me in this project, as well as the high school teachers and students who participated in this research. I would also like to express my gratitude to editor Sun Mingli from Sichuan University Press for her enthusiastic assistance in the publication of this book. Due to the limitation of the author, omissions and shortcomings in the book are inevitable, readers are kindly requested to criticize and correct them.

Table of Contents

CHAPTER ONE
INTRODUCTION

1. 1   Introduction

This first chapter began with an overview of the background of the research, and then continued with the problem statement, research objectives, research questions, research hypotheses, conceptual framwork, the significance of the study, the limitation of the study, the operational definitions of the study, and finally, a summary of the current study.

1. 2   Background

Since 2001, the Ministry of Education (MoE) of China has implemented The Rural Primary School Merger Program. The objective of this nationwide program was to officially authorize the closure of smaller schools in faraway villages and reallocate the students to larger schools which were known as " central schools". With the reduced number of schools in the country, the quality of schools could be enhanced by concentrating investment, such as improved facilities and more well-trained teaching staff. Since the start of this major educational reform, the enrollments of village-level rural elementary schools have been greatly reduced. The number was reduced from a total of 41, 698 schools in 2001 to 17, 633 in 2016. The number of rural junior middle schools was 41, 038 in 2001, but this number was reduced to 15,631 by the year 2016 (National Bureau of Statistics, 2016). From the year 2001 to 2016, a total of 25,407 rural junior middle schools in China have been closed (National Bureau of Statistics, 2016).

Therefore, many of the students from countryside schools were sent to boarding schools that were far away from their homes. Due to the rural primary school merger program, most of the rural junior middle school students became school boarders. Since 2015, 1,681,300 students had been relocated to primary and junior middle boarding schools (Wu, 2016).

To be sure, boarding schools have both advantages and disadvantages for boarders. On the bright side, boarding schools provide boarders with more convenience of school amenities, for instance, libraries and sports centers. Boarding schools also provide students with more opportunities to interact with teachers and classmates.

However, from another point of view, boarding schools have been linked to many psychological problems arising from its ecological environment. Firstly, boarders are far away from home, and they are in general, deprived of strong family emotional support. As a result, they usually feel lonely and isolated (Cookson, 2009). Secondly, due to the high student-teacher ratios, the boarders often lack sufficient attention from their new-found guardians (Zai & Xuan, 2011; Yue et al., 2014). Without enough guardians' supervision, boarders have more chance to approach problematic students or underachievers. They may easily imitate mis-behaviors such as bullying, alcohol dependency and smoking (Zhu et al., 2008). Thirdly, it is demonstrated that boarders from China's rural junior middle schools usually have lower academic achievements, compared with non-boarders in junior middle school. Fourthly, and most importantly, researchers have discovered that boarders have psychological well-being issues which were worse than non-hostel students (Murfin, 1977). A survey by Wang et al. (2009), which was based on 4,840 boarders from 38 hostels in rural middle schools in China, found that nearly more than half of rural junior middle school students suffered from psychological health problems.

Furthermore, learning anxiety was the most widespread psychological health issue, according to a survey using the Children's Manifest Anxiety Scale (CMAS). Wang et al. (2015) also revealed that psychological well-being was positively linked to school dropout. The dropout rate of rural junior middle school students with psychological health problems was three times more than that of students without mental health problems. In light of the prevailing situation, whereby most rural junior middle schools in China haven't counselors or psychology teachers, Wang et al. (2015) strongly recommended that the policymakers in education should set up psychological healthcare programs. For example, school counsellors, psychology teachers and psychological well-being classes should be provided in rural junior middle schools.

In addition, rural junior middle school students face other challenges, such as the high frequency rate of one-parent families, or becoming stay-at-home kids after their parents go to work in the cities. The latter have been found to have a greater tendency to drop out of school (Zhang, 2006; Qiao et al., 2008). Furthermore, students in the rural junior middle school have to pass the entrance examination for senior high school before they graduate from junior middle school. The examination achievements of rural junior middle school students were much weaker than that of students from the cities, which had made the former more anxious about their academic abilities in the competitive education system. Hence, this in turn, had led to high learning anxiety and dropout rate.

1. 3   Problem Statement

School dropout is a worldwide issue. For example, 31 percent of students dropped out of the school system in Myanmar (United Nations Educational, Scientific and Cultural Organization [UNESCO], 2012). A similar situation is found in many developing countries. Based on the report of the UNESCO Institute for Statistics, the dropout rate is 32 percent in Tunisia, 17 percent in Paraguay, 25 percent in Honduras and 24 percent in China (Marshall et al., 2014; Shi et al., 2015). In rural China, the average dropout rate between Grade 7 and Grade 8 rural junior middle school students was 13 percent, and ranged from 7.2 percent to 27.1 percent across different counties (Wang et al., 2015).

Li (2017) found that the high dropout rate not only harmed the development of rural education, but also hindered the development of China's economy and brought about many social problems. Firstly, the chances for unskilled labor to find employment would be very slim in the future, as most of the well-paid jobs would require at least a degree or diploma. Secondly, the high dropout rate has been linked to adolescent crime. Xinhua News revealed that nearly half of adolescent crimes were committed by juveniles between the ages 16 and 17, and many of these criminal suspects have been dropouts of the school system. Thirdly, Freudenberg and Ruglis (2007) revealed that education was positively linked to health; the educated people live a healthier life than the less educated. A high student dropout rate leads to more costs for the health care system in the long run. Fourthly, if the dropout rate could not be reduced, there would be a national stability problem, with increasing unemployment and growing disparities between cities and counties. As a result, the whole society in China would beset by more social problems (Wang et al., 2015).

There were many external factors which had caused students to dropout in rural China. The vital extrinsic reason was the issue of economy. There was a positive correlation between high dropout ratios and poverty (Brown & Park, 2002; Filmer, 1999; Boyes, Berg & Cluver, 2017). When the unskilled labor force could get a high salary in the labor market, it would attract the students to work before they had finished school. Furthermore, students faced especially intense pressure of unemployment even after graduation from college. In such a difficult circumstance, the opportunity cost of continuing school was high. In a highly competitive educational system, even if students did not have to pay for tuition and other fees, and if the government even provided free lunch, the dropout rate would still be high (Glewwe & Kremer, 2006).

However, apart from the economic factor, there were many other non-economic factors which contributed to the high school dropout rate in rural China.

Many demographic variables affect the school dropout rate. Several studies have revealed that students with all of the following demographic characteristics were more prone to drop out: boys who were older than 14 years old, studying in Grade 8, living in a boarding school, showing poor academic performance, having more siblings, whose father had less education and low family income (Li, Zang & An, 2013; Wang et al., 2015).

Beyond the above extrinsic factors, there were also intrinsic considerations which might lead to a high student dropout rate. Psychological health issues were widely distributed amongst rural students; for example, some rural junior middle school students have been found to suffer from mental health problems. Dropping out was positively linked to poor psychological health (Shi et al., 2015). Psychological health issues affecting particularly poor students with low achievement, were a major cause of the high dropout rate among rural junior middle school students in China (Shi et al., 2015). The students with more psychological health problems were three times more prone to drop out, compared with students with less psychological health problems.

Among the types of psychological health problems faced by Chinese students, learning anxiety was the most serious prevailing problem and the major cause of dropout rates (Wang et al., 2015). Many other researchers have also presented that learning anxiety was positively linked to dropout rates among students with low achievement.

Although learning anxiety is a vital factor which affects students' psychological health, and in turn, dropout rate, it is an expensive endeavor to try to change extrinsic factors, such as students' economic situation and demographic factors, as a means to address the problem. However, it is easier and more cost-effective to implement some positive psychological interventions to reduce students' learning anxiety and dropout rate.

If students can improve their social emotional techniques, they can better handle their daily problems and live a better and more successful life (CASEL, 2017). Schools are the best sites to address such social and emotional problems and support students' socio-emotional development. This is because students spend most of their time in schools (Durlak et al., 2011), especially for the boarding school students.

Even if schools have implemented a psychological healthcare service, the resources needed for each individual student are still an issue. Schools have not given the proper attention to students who have psychological health issues. The same situation is also found in China. There is simply not enough psychological health prevention and intervention measures in rural junior middle schools. Li (2017) has pointed out that there were no psychology teachers and no psychological well-being classes in many rural junior middle schools. The study further argued that to meet the requirements of psychological health prevention and intervention for rural junior middle school students, there should be a pedagogical framework to guide the provision of school-based psychological healthcare services (Li, 2017).

A Social and Emotional Learning (SEL) course, which is aimed at widespread delivery, is a Tier Ⅰ effort within the Multi-tiered Systems of Support (MTSS). MTSS is an evidence-based academic framework. It adheres to a compatible, complete, and structural design to meet students' academic, social and behavioral needs (Benner et al., 2013; Moretti, 2010). An effective MTSS would include different, but compatible and consistent levels of intervention, such as embedded protocols, required steps, and school-wide stimulators (Benner et al., 2013; Cowen, 1994). Tier Ⅰ efforts include core instruction and systemic protocols that will be able to satisfy all students' requirements. Tier Ⅱ efforts are set up to help students who are in danger of having difficulties to meet the behavior requirements at school. Finally, Tier Ⅲ efforts are especially helpful for those students who do not have the foundational techniques to fulfill the requirements of academic or behavioral outcomes by grade level at school (Horner & Sugai, 2015).

SEL intervention has been for a long time widely implemented in many countries, such as the USA and England. Nevertheless, it has only begun to make its presence felt in China (Li, Yang & Huang, 2018). There are two reported SEL interventions in China at present: one is initiated by the Ministry of Education in China (MoE) and the other one by The United Nations Children's Fund (Li, et al. , 2018). The former official program used a curriculum adapted from supportive materials provided by the learning behavior center of the University of Northampton. This program consisted of several lessons, including "New start" "Quarrel and reconciliation" "Say No to bullying" "Moving towards the goal" "Like myself", and "Interpersonal relationship and Change". This Social and Emotional Learning (SEL) intervention was delivered by class teachers and main subject teachers. There was one lesson per week, and every grade had a different specific curriculum. The program depended on the cooperation of teachers, parents and schools. This kind of SEL intervention was time-consuming and expensive, and there was no report on whether there was any reduction of student learning anxiety and dropout rate at present.

Another SEL intervention was implemented by Wang et al. (2016), which was specially aimed at reducing student learning anxiety and dropout rate. It was based on a curriculum compiled by an educational psychologist from Beijing Normal University. In this intervention, music, art and physical education teachers were invited to implement the curriculum. Wang et al. (2016) chose the teachers from these three disciplines as they had more spare time, compared with main subject teachers. However, the intended effect was not strong enough. It had reduced leaning anxiety only by 2. 3 percent and dropout rate by 1. 6 percent; while the actual learning anxiety in general was 66 percent and the dropout rate varied from 7. 2 percent to 27. 1 percent across different counties (Wang et al. , 2016).

The weak intervention effect might have been due to several reasons. Firstly, the curriculum was not evidence-based and was implemented for the first time. A school-wide, Tier I SEL curricular tool, such as Strong Kids could have been a better choice for reducing junior middle school students' learning anxiety and dropout rate. The program has been proven to be an evidence-based and cost-effective curriculum, which could improve students' psychological health and tenacity, according to the growth of health ability techniques. It could also

7

reduce students' dropout rate (Hardre & Reeve, 2003).

Secondly, the type of teacher selected to deliver the intervention might also affect the effect on the students. Although Durlak et al. (2011) have revealed that school teachers, in general, were competent to implement the SEL curriculum, the right kind of school teacher to better implement the intervention has not been proven. There were many kinds of school teachers who have been invited to implement the SEL intervention, such as the art teacher, music teacher, physical education teacher, class teacher, and even principals (Merrell et. al, 2010). As the SEL intervention is a kind of psychological health intervention in school. Compared with other kinds of teachers who knew little about psychological knowledge and lacked the experience in delivering psychological intervention, the psychology teacher who has a background in psychological intervention, may have the relevant knowledge and be more familiar with the correct techniques for carrying out a SEL intervention (Li, 2017).

Thirdly, the pedagogical approach in delivering the SEL intervention by teachers might also affect the learning outcome. Hetrick (2018) found that a SEL intervention required some modification to improve student engagement and enhance expected results. Jang, Reeve and Deci (2010) found that teacher autonomy support could create a warm and democratic environment for students to learn and improve engagement. Harlacher and Merrell (2010) found that praise and positive feedback were effective in improving students' SEL knowledge and use of SEL techniques. Praise and positive feedback were examples of instructional support based on the tenets of teacher autonomy support (Reeve & Jang, 2006).

Reeve and Jang (2006) identified six teacher autonomy support instructional behaviors, include "Asking what students want" "Giving students' time to learn in the way they like" "Applauding as feedback" "Explaining reasons" "Providing encouragement" and "Offering clues". Furthermore, Jang, Reeve and Halusic (2016) found that watching video clips and having whole-group discussions could satisfy students' need for autonomy and improve their learning capacity.

Reeve (1998) found that teacher autonomy support was teachable. Cheon,

Reeve, and Lee (2018) implemented the Autonomy Support Intervention Program (ASIP) to train teachers the autonomy supportive teaching styles. However, it has not been identified yet that whether delivering SEL in a teacher autonomy supportive way can significantly reduce student dropout rate.

To sum up, the boarding school merger program has resulted in rural junior middle school students experiencing a high rate of psychological health problems, especially with regard to learning anxiety and dropout intention. At present, "reducing dropout" in Chinese rural elementary education has become an urgent task for the Ministry of Education. There should be proper effective intervention measures to control the school dropout problem. Based on the weak effect of existing SEL interventions on reducing the dropout rate, it is extremely urgent to have much more effective intervention measures to improve retention and reduce the dropout rate among rural junior middle school students in rural China. In light of the literature review carried out for this study, it was proposed that a modified SEL intervention, a Teacher Autonomy Supportive SEL intervention, which was based on Strong Kids curriculum, might be an appropriate approach to tackle the issue at hand.

First of all, in China, there is no SEL intervention based on the Strong Kids curriculum, especially the Strong Kids Intervention Grade 6 – 8 (Carrizales-Engelmannet al., 2016). This version has been proven to be an evidence-based and cost-effective prevention and early intervention measure for Tier Ⅰ intervention (Tereza, 2018). In the present study, Strong Kids Intervention Grade 6 – 8 would, for the first time, be used in the rural junior middle school setting in southwest of China. At this research site, the study first explored whether the Strong Kids Intervention Grade 6 – 8 could improve the rural junior middle school students' SEL knowledge, reduce learning anxiety and dropout intention. Harlacher and Merrell (2010) have claimed that the SEL intervention, as implemented in other countries and cultures, had the same effect in different cultures.

In the present study, the dropout intention was used to predict the dropout rate, as it has been proven that the dropout intention could predict the actual dropout rate for up to one year (Eicher et al. , 2014).

Secondly, although Harlacher and Merrell (2010) provided some evidence to suggest that teacher autonomy support was important in delivering a SEL intervention. Furthermore, Herrick (2018) suggested that more modification of the SEL intervention was required. However, there has not yet been a systematically modified SEL intervention through a teacher autonomy supportive pedagogical method, and the training of teachers on how to deliver a SEL intervention in a teacher autonomy supportive way, such as using Autonomy Support Intervention Program (ASIP) (Cheon et al. , 2015).

Cheon et al. (2015) explained that the ASIP would have to include three important steps. The first step was to inform teachers about the importance of autonomy support teaching in class. The second step was to train the teachers to acquire the techniques on how to use teacher autonomy supportive instructions in class, such as "provide structure for the study" "Praise as information feedback" "Provide rationales" "Offering encouragement", and "Offering hints". The third and last step was to ask teachers to share their own experience in using teacher autonomy supportive instruction behaviors in their class, and the obstacles they faced when they practiced a teacher autonomy supportive instructional approach.

In the current study, for the purpose of comparing the effect of SEL intervention and TASSEL intervention on rural junior middle school students' SEL knowledge, learning anxiety and dropout intention, six teacher autonomy supportive instructional behaviors were added as the teachers' repertoire when they were delivering the original Strong Kids curriculum. These six teacher autonomy supportive instructional behaviors include the following, "Allowing students to choose seats and sit with their friends" "Providing structure for each lesson" "Asking students to share their own experiments and accept students' negative emotions" "Asking students to draw or write about their feeling" "Giving rationales and appraise activities according to the lesson", and "Allowing group discussions with teamwork".

Thirdly, it has not been determined yet what kind of school teachers would be more suitable to implement the SEL intervention. Even though Durlak et al. (2011) have proven that school teachers in general would be competent to deliver a SEL intervention, the issue remained with regard to the appropriate choice of school teachers to effectively deliver the SEL intervention. As psychology teachers have the educational psychology background and necessary practical experience in delivering psychological healthcare activities, it is only logical to assume that psychology teachers would be the better choice to deliver a Strong Kids curriculum, compared with the use of regular school teachers.

The Strong Kids curriculum is based on Emotional Intelligence theory and cognitive behavior theory. This curriculum has an idea that when students improve their SEL knowledge, it will change their mind and reduce negative emotion and behavior, and the Strong Kids curriculum include SEL knowledge and skill teaching. SEL also invented their own SEL knowledge test. Tran (2007) revealed that a Strong Kids SEL intervention could help reduce student SEL symptoms and improve SEL knowledge and social emotional techniques. Eicher et al. (2014) pointed out that dropout intention could forecast students' actual dropout behavior in one year. Therefore, in this research dropout intention was used to test students' intention to drop out of the school system, as well as the student dropout rate.

Nevertheless, The best combination of teacher type and intervention type to improve SEL knowledge and reduce students learning anxiety and dropout intention has not been identified. As a result, in this research, we will use 2 × 2 design to find out the best combination of intervention group to implement Strong Kids based on SEL intervention.

1. 4   Research Objectives

This research investigated the effects of varying teacher type and intervention type on students' SEL knowledge, learning anxiety and dropout intention when delivering a Strong Kids curriculum at a junior middle school in rural southwest of

China. To achieve this target, there were eight particular study objectives.

Ⅰ. To examine if there is significant main effect of teacher type (RT vs PT) on the combination of SEL Knowledge, learning anxiety and dropout intention at posttest.

Ⅱ. To examine if there is significant main effect of intervention type (SEL vs TASSEL) on the combination of SEL knowledge, learning anxiety and dropout intention at posttest.

Ⅲ. To examine if there is significant interaction effect of teacher type (RT vs PT) and intervention type (SEL vs TASSEL) on the combination of SEL knowledge, learning anxiety and dropout intention at posttest.

Ⅳ. To examine if there is significant main effect of groups on the combination of SEL knowledge, learning anxiety and dropout intention among four groups from pretest to posttest.

Ⅴ. To examine if there is significant main effect of time on the combination of SEL knowledge, learning anxiety and dropout intention from pretest to posttest in each group.

Ⅵ. To examine if there is significant interaction effect of Time × Group on the combination of SEL knowledge, learning anxiety and dropout intention from pretest to posttest.

Ⅶ. To examine if the present intervention is effective to reduce rural junior middle school students' learning anxiety percentage from pretest to posttest.

Ⅷ. To examine if the present intervention is effective to reduce rural junior middle school students' dropout intention percentage from pretest to posttest.

1.5 Research Questions

Based on our research objectives, there are eight corresponding research questions.

Ⅰ. Is there any significant main effect of teacher type (RT vs PT) on the combination of SEL knowledge, learning anxiety and dropout intention at posttest?

II. Is there any significant main effect of intervention type (SEL vs TASSEL) on the combination of SEL knowledge, learning anxiety and dropout intention at posttest?

III. Is there any significant interaction effect of teacher type (RT vs PT) and intervention type (SEL vs TASSEL) on the combination of SEL knowledge, learning anxiety and dropout intention at posttest?

IV. Is there any significant main effect of groups on the combination of SEL Knowledge, learning anxiety and dropout intention among four groups from pretest to posttest?

V. Is there any significant main effect of time on the combination of SEL knowledge, learning anxiety and dropout intention from pretest to posttest in each group?

VI. Is there any significant interaction effect of Time × Group on the combination of SEL knowledge, learning anxiety and dropout intention from pretest to posttest?

VII. Is the present intervention effective in reducing rural junior middle school students' learning anxiety percentage from pretest to posttest?

VIII. Is the present intervention effective in reducing rural junior middle school students' dropout intention percentage from pretest to posttest?

1.6 Research Hypotheses

Based on our research objectives and research questions, there are eight corresponding research hypotheses.

H1: There is significant main effect of teacher type (RT vs PT) on the combination of SEL knowledge, learning anxiety and dropout intention at posttest.

H2: There is significant main effect of intervention type (SEL vs TASSEL) on the combination of SEL knowledge, learning anxiety and dropout intention at posttest.

H3: There is significant interaction effect of teacher type (RT vs PT) and intervention type (SEL vs TASSEL) on the combination of SEL knowledge, learning anxiety and dropout intention at posttest.

H4: There is significant main effect of groups on the combination of SEL knowledge, learning anxiety and dropout intention among four groups from pretest to posttest.

H5: There is significant main effect of time on the combination of SEL knowledge, learning anxiety and dropout intention from pretest to posttest in each group.

H6: There is significant interaction effect of Time × Group on the combination of SEL knowledge, learning anxiety and dropout intention from pretest to posttest.

H7: The present intervention is effective to reduce rural junior middle school students' learning anxiety percentage from pretest to posttest.

H8: The present intervention is effective to reduce rural junior middle school students' dropout intention percentage from pretest to posttest.

1.7 Conceptual Framework

In this study, the conceptual framework is grounded in two main theories: One is the Emotional Intelligence (EI) theory, and the other is Self-Determination Theory (SDT). Emotional Intelligence refers to "the awareness of our emotions and the importance of the emotions play in our relationships and our lives" (Goleman, 1995; Salovey & Mayer, 1990; Baron, 1997). There are three variants of EI theories, namely, ability EI model, trait EI model, and mixed EI model. Social and Emotional Learning (SEL) is based on Goleman's (2002) Mixed Model of EI theory (CASEL, 2017).

Goleman's (2002) Mixed EI model has claimed that emotional intelligence was derived from the following four competencies: self-awareness competency, self-management competency, social awareness competency, and relationship management competency. In the current study, SEL was defined as "the procedure for both kids and grown-ups to master and validly utilize the science, manners, and techniques essential to comprehend and control sentiments, establish and pursue affirmative objectives, experience and express compassion for other people, build and retain affirmative relationships, and put forward reliable decisions" (CASEL, 2017).

There have been many different kinds of SEL interventions implemented in different countries. Durlak et al. (2011) found that students generally improved their SEL techniques and decreased their internal and external problem behaviors. Even so, the present SEL intervention program in China was not effective enough to reduce the rural junior middle school dropout rate. It could only reduce the dropout rate by 1.6 percent, while the actual dropout rate was more than 20 percent. Therefore, there is an urgent need to improve the effectiveness of SEL intervention and to reduce the student dropout rates (Wang, 2016). In this regard, an evidence-based, cost-effective SEL intervention, which was called the Strong Kids program was introduced in China for the first time with the aim of reducing student dropout rates (Merrell et al. , 2008).

Tran (2007) revealed that a Strong Kids SEL intervention could help reduce student SEL symptoms and improve SEL knowledge and social emotional techniques. Wang et al. (2016) found that a SEL intervention had the capacity to decrease learning anxiety and dropout rate. Eicher et al. (2014) pointed out that dropout intention could forecast students' actual dropout behavior in one year. Therefore, in this research, dropout intention was used to test students' intention to drop out of the school system, as well as the student dropout rate.

The other theory which was adopted as a conceptual framework for the current study was the Self-determination Theory (SDT). SDT was an extensive analytical framework for studying human motivation and personality (Deci & Ryan, 2008). SDT expounds the meta theory of constructing motivation research, defines the formal theory of internal motivation and various external motivation sources, and describes the respective roles of intrinsic motivation and extrinsic motivation types in cognitive and social development. The theory deals with how social and cultural factors promote or weaken people's willpower and initiative, as well as their well-being and work quality.

From the perspective of SDT, conditions that support individual experience of autonomy, ability and relationship are considered to cultivate the most willpower and high-quality activity motivation and participation forms, including improving performance, persistence and creativity. Furthermore, Deci & Ryan (2008) argued that the principles of the SDT also operated in the social environment. If the three mental requirements mentioned above were not met, there would be an intense harmful impact on the health of the social environment.

According to the SDT, students have three essential psychological demands, the first demand is autonomy, the second demand is competence, and the third demand is relatedness (Deci & Ryan, 2008). If these three needs are met, the probability of students' dropping out of school is low. Teacher autonomy support has been proven to satisfy students' basic needs in class and reduce the dropout rate (Hardre & Reeve, 2003; Vallerand et al., 1997).

Varelland et al. (1997) also found that Teacher Autonomy Support (TAS) could arouse students' intrinsic motivation and assist in reducing their dropout rate. Harlacher and Merrell (2010) provided evidence to suggest that teacher autonomy support could be useful in delivering a SEL intervention. However, it has not shown how to systematically train teachers on how to deliver a SEL intervention in a teacher autonomy supportive way. Furthermore, which kind of teacher is the better choice to deliver the SEL intervention has not been determined yet.

Therefore, in this research, different intervention types, Social and Emotional Learning (SEL) intervention and Teacher Autonomy Supportive Social and Emotional Learning (TASSEL) intervention were used to compare their different impacts on students' SEL knowledge, learning anxiety and dropout intention. In addition, two different types of teachers (psychology teacher and regular teacher) were compared to see their effect on SEL knowledge, learning anxiety and dropout intention. In addition, we want to see the best combination of teacher type and intervention type on improving SEL knowledge, and reducing learning anxiety and dropout intention. Hence, with a 2 × 2 factorial design, there were four treatments in the present study, and each group has pretest and posttest. The conceptual framework of the present research is as shown in Figure 1. 1.

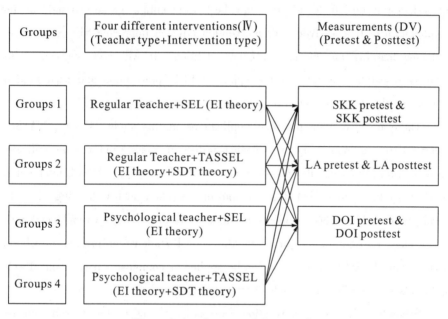

Figure 1. 1 Conceptual framework

1. 8 The Significance of the Study

This study has both theoretical and practical significance. There are three theoretical implication in this study. Firstly, we developed teacher autonomy supportive social and emotional learning intervention, which is called TASSEL intervention particularly for Chinese rural junior middle school students. As this TASSEL intervention is based on survey of Chinese culture and how to add teacher autonomy supportive instructions to existing SEL intervention, which made it a new intervention and suitable for Chinese researchers to adapt in future research.

Secondly, we also translated SEL knowledge and dropout intention instruments based on back-to-back translation, which will give Chinese researchers the corresponding instruments to apply when they want to check the intervention effect with pretest and posttest.

Thirdly, in order to have more robust intervention effect, we used a 2×2 quasi-factorial design to identify the best intervention group, based on the combination of teacher type and intervention type on improving SEL knowledge, reducing learning anxiety and dropout intention. It will give suggestions for Chinese researchers about how to implement SEL intervention and what kind of teacher to choose according to needed intervention purpose.

There are also three practical implications in this study. Firstly, TASSEL intervention as a compulsory psychological well-being class which can be replicated in other rural junior middle schools in China. In this study, TASSEL intervention was successfully implemented as compulsory psychological well-being class for rural junior middle school students in China. As there is no psychological well-being class curriculum for junior middle school students at present in China. Hence, the TASSEL intervention can be applied as compulsory psychological well-being class for junior middle school students in China.

Secondly, TASSEL intervention can assist China to foster well-educated citizens and maintain national stability by reducing students' dropout. As rural junior middle school dropout may induce less-educated citizens and ruin national stability between cities and counties, so it is urgent for Chinese government to reduce rural junior middle school students' dropout and foster well-educated citizens and maintain national stability by reducing students' dropout. TASSEL intervention with psychology teacher is successful in reducing students' dropout, which can be widely implemented in China.

Thirdly, the current study is aimed at advising educational policymakers to pay more attention to the cultivation of students' emotional intelligence and implement TASSEL intervention in junior middle schools in China. As emotional intelligence plays a vital role in adolescent development, and TASSEL intervention is particularly to improve students' emotional intelligence. Therefore, the present study will give strong advice to policymakers to pay more attention to the cultivation of students' emotional intelligence and implement TASSEL intervention in junior middle schools in China.

1. 9　The Limitations of the Study

Firstly, the study employed a factorial design whereby intact groups (i. e., classrooms) were assigned the treatment condition, and participants were distributed to each intervention group at random. Owing to the non-random distribution, the intervention group may be unequal in certain variables and therefore, not within the control of the researcher. Secondly, it would be inappropriate to extrapolate the results of the present study to the altogether different situation of junior middle schools in rich or metropolitan regions in China. Thirdly, the context of intervention is only intervention at the classroom level, and not at the level of the school and neighborhood. Therefore, it lacks understanding of the program effect at the broader ecological perspective. Fourthly, although the dropout intention will greatly predict actual dropout rate, due to the time limitation of this study to measure the actual dropout rate, the students' intention to drop out from school was used as the dependent variable. Ideally, it would have been the optimal solution that includes both the dropout intention and actual dropout rate in a longitudinal study.

1. 10　The Operational Definitions

The following operational definitions of variables for this research were derived from a literature review of previous studies in educational contexts.

1. 10. 1　SEL knowledge

SEL knowledge refers to knowledge of wholesome social-emotional behavioral techniques, particularly the notions taught in the Strong Kids courses.

The 20-items self-report knowledge questionnaire was designed to assess the knowledge of healthy social emotional and behavioral techniques before and after the test, especially the concepts taught in the Strong Kids Course (see Appendix C). Knowledge questionnaire is essentially a way to measure students' knowledge, especially social and emotional coping strategies and knowledge, by reflecting the content taught in the course.

These items consist of true and false items and multiple selection items. Each item is scored correctly or incorrectly using the scoring keys provided in the course. Correct answer gets 1 point for each question, correct completion of all test questions up to 20 points. The final correct score can be converted to the percentage of correct answers. Examples include: marking right or wrong — "Self-esteem is your sense of value to yourself", multiple choices — "An example of uncomfortable emotions for most people is (a) excitement, (b) frustration, (c) curiosity, (d) content".

1. 10. 2　Junior High Dropout

Junior high dropout refers to a student who has left the school system without completing the required period of study, i. e. , fulfilling the condition that a student will be enrolled in junior middle school from Grade 7 to 9 (Wang et al. , 2016).

1. 10. 3　Junior High Dropout Intention

Junior high dropout intention refers to the students' intention to drop out of the school system before finishing the required period of study, i. e. , fulfilling the condition that a student will be enrolled in junior middle school from Grade 7 to 9 (Varelland et al. , 1997).

This scale was used to test rural junior middle school students' intention to dropout. It includes two items to assess the willingness to stick to school or drop out. From Vallerand et al. (1997), sample items are "I sometimes think about dropping out" and "I intend to drop out". Each item uses a six-point Likert-type scale ranging from 1 (strongly disagreed) to 6 (strongly agreed). In the Vallerand et al. (1997) survey, the two items are highly correlated with each other. One year later, the questionnaire predicts actual dropout behavior, which is sensitive to students' motivation. A third inquiry about continuing education intention was added to the questionnaire (see Appendix E). "Sometimes I feel uncertain about continuing to study year after year. " A score more than 9 means students have dropout intention (Hardre & Reeve, 2003).

1.10.4   Learning Anxiety

Learning anxiety is defined as a systematic fear or worry about school activities, accompanied by emotional distress (Barrios & Hartmann, 1997; Spielberger & Vagg, 1995). It consists of 15 questions included in the Mental Health Test (MHT) (Gan, Bi & Ruan, 2007; Zhou, 1991). Each item uses a "yes" or "no" answer. Correct answer gets 1 point for each question, correct completion of all test questions up to 15 points. More than 8 points on this variable implies higher levels of learning anxiety, less than 3 indicates low level of learning anxiety (Yao et al. , 2011).

1.10.5   Social and Emotional Learning (SEL)

Social and emotional learning is defined as "the procedure for both kids and grown-ups to foster necessary techniques to identify and manage sentiments, cultivate empathy, be responsible for decision making, maintain positive interpersonal relations, and successfully address the needs of growth in the complicated modern society" (CASEL, 2017).

1. 10. 6　Teacher Autonomy Support

Teacher autonomy support refers to instructional behavior in an academic environment where instructors promote consistency by distinguishing and fostering student requirements, taste and preferences (Reeve, 2006).

1. 10. 7　TASSEL Intervention

Teacher autonomy supportive social and emotional learning intervention refers to a pedagogical approach whereby SEL intervention occurs in an academic environment in which instructors promote consistency by distinguishing and fostering student requirements, taste and preferences.

1. 11　Summary

This chapter first described the background of the rural junior middle school merger program in China, followed by a discussion of the psychological health issues brought about by this policy, especially on two issues in this study, i. e., student learning anxiety and high dropout rate. The present studies have provided empirical evidence that this problematic state in the boarding schools was the result of its ecological system, and they have recommended measures that a school-based psychological healthcare service should be adopted in order to address the central issues and thus, solve the problem.

CHAPTER TWO
LITERATURE REVIEW

2. 1　Introduction

This chapter elaborated the brief literature review according to the variables of the study. It began with the background and reasons for rural junior middle school students' dropout and requirement for psychological intervention and prevention to reduce rural junior middle school students' dropout intention. It also introduced Multi-tiered Systems of Support (MTSS) to psychological health, and Social and Emotional Learning (SEL) programs as Tier I intervention to psychological health, especially Strong Kids series intervention. At last, based on the limitation of present SEL intervention, especially Strong Kids intervention to reduce dropout, this research discussed the improvement of Strong Kids intervention to reduce rural junior middle school students' dropout intention, and followed by conceptual framework of this study, significance and development of TASSEL intervention and the summary of this chapter.

2. 2　The Effects of School Merger on Rural Junior Middle School Students

At the beginning of 2000, one of the most protruding tasks of the Ministry of Education (MoE) in China was to implement the rural primary school merger plan

(Luo et al. , 2009). In current years, the enrollments of rural elementary schools at village level have greatly declined, from 41,698 schools in the year of 2001 to 17,633 schools in the year of 2016, and the quantity of rural junior middle schools reduced from 41,038 in the year of 2001 to 15,631 in the year of 2016 (National Bureau of Statistics, 2016). Correspondingly, the Merger Program started to shut down smaller schools in quite faraway thorps and combined them into larger "central" schools. From year 2001 to year 2016, a number of 25, 407 Chinese rural junior middle schools have been closed (National Bureau of Statistics, 2016). Accordingly, a lot of rural students transferred to boarding schools, which are distant from their homes. Since the carrying out of the elementary school merger program, there are a growing number of boarding school students, which are called boarders. Since 2015, there have been 1,681,300 boarding students in primary and junior middle schools (Wu, 2016). MoE believed that with the decrease of schools, the quality of establishment and faculties could be improved more efficaciously through centralized investment.

Honestly and obviously, there are many advantages of boarding schools. First of all, compared to non-boarders, boarding schools provide more time for boarding students to use school facilities such as libraries and gymnasiums (Shu & Tong, 2015; Adetunj, 2007). There are also more chances for boarding students to discuss and learn from peers and instructors.

Moreover, lodging schools provide boarding students with more opportunities to emulate fine social norms, which can help them better handle emotional problems and amend their bad behaviors. For instance, roommates who live in the same dormitory can teach disadvantaged and problematic students or demonstrate better lifestyle choices to help them accommodate to the harshness of intellectual life (Bronfenbrenner, 1970; Adams, 1995; Papworth, 2014; Xu et al. , 2000).

However, there are also many shortcomings of boarding schools in rural China. Boarding schools may induce some passive effects on students. On one hand, boarders may lose their parents' care and support when they leave their safe family circumstance (Cookson, 2009). Combined with vulnerable sustain system, it is more likely for boarders to result in social isolation (Ak & Sayil, 2006).

On the other hand, boarders are also inclined to take passive actions. For example, they may foster bad habits of drinking alcohol, smoking cigarettes, fighting with other students, etc. The reason behind this is that they are easily exposed to problematic students or students with poor grades and habits (Zhu et al. , 2008). At the same time, boarders may lack close guardian supervision. For instance, the high ratio of students to teachers shows that teachers do not have enough time and valid ways to solve students' problematic issues (Moswela, 2006; Zai & Xuan, 2011; Yue et al. , 2014).

In addition, the hostel school living condition is usually not so good. There are not enough equipped living quarters (Luo et al. , 2009; Pang & Han, 2005; Lu, 2009; Wang & Li, 2009), and the food in the canteen may have not enough nutrition for the students (Luo et al. , 2009).

Simultaneously, rural junior middle school students have other challenges to face with, such as high frequency rate of single-parent families or become left-behind children after their parents go to work in the cities (Zhang, 2006; Qiao et al. , 2008). Moreover, students in junior middle school have to pass the high school entrance examination (HSEE) before they finish junior middle school (Loyalka et al. , 2013). Based on the poor study environment and low-quality teaching, the academic performance of rural junior middle school students is worse than that of city students (Luo et al. , 2012), which makes them more anxious about their competitive abilities in the competitive education system, and whether they can successfully pass the HSEE and then go on with their study for high school (Yi et al. , 2012).

2.3 Rural Junior Middle School Students' Dropout Rate and Learning Anxiety

For many developing countries, dropping out of junior middle school is a big problem. In this study, junior middle school dropout refers to leaving school system before finishing their study, provided that they are enrolled in junior middle schools (in most developing countries, usually Grades 7 to 9) (Vallerand et al., 1997). For example, in Myanmar, 31 percent of children enrolled in junior middle school depart from school before completion (United Nations Educational, Scientific and Cultural Organization [UNESCO], 2012). This figure is high in many other developing nations. Based on the statistics of the UNESCO Institute (2012), Tunisia is an extreme, where 32 percent of junior middle school dropouts occur; another case is Paraguay, the dropout rate is 17 percent. Honduras has a drop out rate of 25 percent (Marshall et al., 2014). The cumulative dropout rate for all secondary education windows could be as high as 63 percent in rural China (Shi et al., 2015).

According to Wang et al. (2015), the average two-year dropout rate for seventh and eighth grades is 13 percent, and the drop out rate in different schools range from 7.2 percent to 27.1 percent. Furthermore, they believe that some of the rural students confront the danger of psychological health issues. This ratio is 12 higher than that of city students. Among the subclasses of the Mental Health Test, learning anxiety is proven to be the most at-risk cause to dropout rate. Wang et al. (2015) also found that, in addition to gender, the same demographic characteristics of students (older, lower school performance, poor family context) are more dangerous of dropping out of school and have more psychological health issues.

Finally, even without considering the characteristics of students and their families, psychological health issues are still positively linked to dropout rates (Wang et al., 2015). For every standard deviation added to mental heath test, the dropout rate increased by 0. 9 percentage points (Wang et al. , 2015). These relevant results show great significance. Even though these findings are mainly concentrated in impoverished rural junior middle schools, the survey results still provide important factors affecting rural dropouts in China, which may exceed traditional factors.

In this study, learning anxiety is defined as a systematic fear or worry about school activities, accompanied by emotional distress (Barrios & Hartmann, 1997; Spielberger & Vagg, 1995). Learning anxiety also includes exam anxiety, which is a special kind of learning anxiety (McDonald, 2001). After graduate from junior high school, students in China have to pass the High School Entrance Examination (HSEE).

Like other undeveloped areas, high risk and competition from examination systems increase students' anxiety (Liu et al. , 2009; Reddy & Sinha, 2010). For example, a group of junior high school students in remote areas of Shaanxi Province were followed up and investigated by Song et al. (2013). They revealed that HSEE has a strong competitiveness: under the condition of junior middle school graduation, only 41. 9 percent of the students have high school qualifications.

Some other students either continue their study in vocational high school (25 percent), or go to find a job directly (19. 3 percent), or stay in junior middle school for one more year to improve the academic score to meet the Entrance Requirements (13. 8 percent). Wang et al. (2015) argued that when psychological health issue improves one standard deviation (SD), the dropout ratio will increase 0. 9 percent, even after they have controlled the fixed effect of schools and the background characteristics of students. There are also other studies which indicate the similar results (Chen et al. , 2000; McLeod & Kaiser, 2004).

As psychological health problem, especially learning anxiety is a great factor which leads to students' dropout, although it is difficult and expensive to change extrinsic factors such as students' economic situation and demographic factors to reduce dropout, there are still some easy and cost-effective psychological interventions to conduct to reduce students' dropout intention.

2. 4　Multi-tiered Systems of Support（MTSS）to Psychological Health

Multi-tiered Systems of Support（MTSS）is academically validated, evidence-based framework that follows a consistent, comprehensive, and structural design to meet the academic, social and behavioral needs of all students（Benner et al., 2013; Cook et al., 2015; Schwartz, 2016）. MTSS is shown in Figure 2.1.

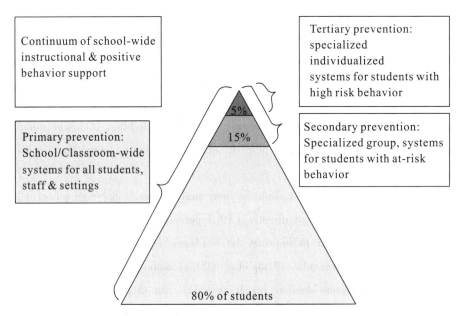

Figure 2. 1　Three-tiered Triangle of support for emotional
and behavior problems（Costello & Angold, 2000）

Effective MTSS contains predictable and consistent tiered intervention. It also embodies whole-school embedded agreement, processes, and incentives（Benner et al., 2013; Cowen, 1994）. Tier I curriculum includes core teaching and system protocols designed to meet the academic needs of all students. Tier II work plan aims to meet the needs of students who may be lower than the grade level or difficult to meet behavioral expectations. Lastly, Tier III intervention is designed particularly for students who may lack the grade level required to achieve the desired academic or behavioral performance (Horner & Sugai, 2015). Multi-tiered Systems of Support (MTSS) provides a systematic approach to prevent, reverse, and reduce mental health challenges through evidence-based practices and behavioral and academic progress monitoring (Cook et al. , 2015).

2. 5   Social and Emotional Learning (SEL) Programs

2. 5. 1   Emotion Intelligence Theory

Emotional intelligence commonly refers to realizing "our sentiments and the significant role of emotion plays in our interpersonal relationship and daily life" (Goleman, 1995; Salovey & Mayer, 1990; Baron, 1997). Thorndike (1920) introduced emotional intelligence as social intelligence and followed the same research route. Gardner (1983) proposed multiple intelligence model, which includes both intrapersonal intelligence and interpersonal intelligence. Based on Thorndike (1920) and Gardner (1983) theories, EI experts developed new models of EI theories. Basically, emotional intelligence experts have brought about three main emotional intelligence (EI) theory models, which are ability EI model, trait EI model, and mixed EI model.

EI competence model includes four contents, including perception of emotions, promotion of thinking, comprehending of emotions and administration of sentiments (Mayer, Salovey & Caruso, 2004). On the contrary, EI trait model regards EI as an emotionally related tendency and has a lower level of EI than the personality traits which determine how human beings behave in a sentimental environment (Petrides, Pita & Kokkinaki, 2007).

In addition to the above two theories, there are mixed EI models, for instance, Bar-on's Emotional Social Intelligence (ESI) model (Bar-on, 2006) and Goleman's Emotional Ability Model (Boyatzis, Goleman & Rhee, 2000), which contain other non-cognitive characteristics, like social skills, motivation, self-respect and individual character.

The present study is in view of Goleman's Mixed EI Model which studies sentimental and social function of individuals. Mixed EI model theory displays multiple conceptualizations of mixed emotional intelligence ability and traits and serves as the underpinning theory for the development of student's adjustment. This mixed EI model considers emotional intelligence as a pack of sentimental and social abilities consisting of cognitive ability and personality. They believe that emotional intelligence comes from four abilities: self-awareness, self-management, social awareness and relationship management.

2.5.2　Development of CASEL and SEL

In 1994, Daniel Goleman, a renowned EI expert, and his colleagues founded the Collaborative for Academic, Social and Emotional Learning Collaboration (CASEL) at a conference sponsored by the Fetzer Institute. The mission of this organization is to help students have a successful school life by adding Social and Emotional Learning (SEL) course to their existing school system. The SEL experts introduce SEL curriculum as a framework to help the students to coordinate it with other courses in school.

For CASEL, it includes the development of evidence-based curriculum benchmarks from preschool to senior school, comprehending and promoting regional and school implementation, and conducting research to link SEL with students' academic achievements and other positive outcomes (CASEL, 2017). CASEL is the pioneer, catalyst and cooperator in the research field of social and emotional learning.

SEL is based on Goleman's mixed models of EI (Goleman et al., 2000), except for the four competencies. SEL adds responsible decision-making as another competency. Therefore, there are five vital capabilities of SEL.

Self-awareness refers to an individual's ability to decide his/her own advantages and challenges with confidence and make positive choices with confidence when dealing with adverse situations. Self-management refers to the capacity to adjust sentiments, reactions, and affections to satisfy the requirement of daily interactivities. Social awareness refers to the ability of perspective taking, comprehending the emotion of other individuals, and differences in values. Relationship skills refer to the capability to build and retain affirmative relationships. Responsible decision-making refers to the ability to care about oneself and other people, and then make decisions with responsibility.

2.5.3   Social and Emotional Learning (SEL) Course

Social and emotional learning course with the purpose of widespread execution is supposed as a Tier I effort under Multi-tiered Systems of Support (MTSS). SEL has been promoted as a way to solve various techniques to improve social emotional ability (Carrizales-Engelmann et al., 2016; Harlacher & Merrell, 2010). SEL intervention is a practicable and promising program to reduce internalizing symptoms and improve interpersonal skills (Kopelman-Rubin et al., 2021).

When the current study is concerned, we applied the definition of SEL from Collaborative for Academic, Social and Emotional Learning (CASEL, 2000). SEL in this study refers to "the procedure through which both kids and grown-ups master and validly utilize the knowledge, manners, and techniques essential to comprehend and control sentiments, set up and pursue affirmative objectives, experience and express compassion for other people, build and retain affirmative relationships, and put forward reliable decisions" (Para 2).

Following the publication of two substantive meta-analysis reviews, containing greater than 500 separate studies of SEL courses, Durlak et al. (2011) confidently suggest adding universal SEL to core teaching (such as mathematics, reading, writing, science). Their analysis confirmed that, in addition to the academic core, when schools concentrate on social and emotional health, in addition to personal emotional health and self-regulation ability, there are also systematic advantages (i.e., school atmosphere, prosocial relations and better school record).

According to Caldarella et al. (2009), it is significant to add SEL course in school, as it is a common issue faced by students, they discovered that "more than three quarters of students do not get enough mental health treatment as what they need at school" (p. 52). Combined with the study on risk and elasticity by Doll and Lyon's (1998), the meta-analysis results of CASEL (2017) and Durlak et al. (2011) announced that schools are the most appropriate place to provide SEL, because they are able to deal with the routine problems that students face with for a long time. Chen, C., Yang, C., and Nie, Q. (2021) found that school-based SEL intervention is practicable to foster SEL competencies and prevent problematic Internet use among Chinese adolescents.

There are many examples of SEL courses which have been invented and reported based on previous studies. Each project has its own method to fulfil the distinct needs of students for psychological health intervention (Payton et al., 2000). Nevertheless, the benefits from SEL courses depend greatly on the techniques the program hopes to deal with and are consistent with the participants' civilization and demographic structure.

CASEL (2017), Durlak et al. (2011) and Taylor et al. (2017) worked together to analyze the validity of 475 SEL curriculum interventions for K-8 students. CASEL (2017) analyzed the initial stage of research. Durlak et al. (2011) reviewed programs K-12. According to the half a year post hoc data collection from different schools, 231 SEL projects were investigated, Durlak et al. (2011) concluded that students generally showed improved SEL techniques and reduced internalization and externalization actions.

Taylor et al. (2017) made further efforts to analyze the subsequent outcomes of 82 general SEL projects that were conducted in school environment, including 97,000 student participants. Each school was asked to follow a stage wise curriculum plan to improve particular techniques, allowing students to actively learn teaching methods (e. g., role playing, interacting groups), and invest adequate time to develop target techniques. These specific targeted SEL technique development can consistently demonstrate significant personal (e. g., internalization and externalization) and academic benefits (Durlak et al., 2011; Payton et al., 2008; Taylor et al., 2017).

Durlak et al. (2011) found student participants who took part in SEL guidance developed 11 – 17 percent prosocial behavior compared to those who did not receive such intervention. Harlacher and Merrell (2010) revealed that emotional education project can reduce internalizing and externalizing actions. Durlak et al. (2011) further added that SEL can be a great help to improve participants' overall SEL techniques development.

Programming Examples: It is meaningful for the school to choose a course that is suitable for students and can be accessible to both staff and students. Most efficient courses follow the five core competencies of CASEL (2017) as the framework of curriculum development. Several vital SEL programs are outlined below to illustrate the various methods of SEL.

The Incredible Years: Dinosaur Social Skills and Problem Solving Curriculum is a course which lasts two years, has 128-hour lessons for pre-school to third year students (Webster-Stratton & Reid, 2004). There are 2 – 3 classes every week, each class has two parts a day, each part lasts 15 – 20 minutes (Webster-Stratton et al., 2004). The course includes emotional techniques, interpersonal techniques, empathy, anger control, and the way to succeed in school (Webster-Stratton et al., 2004).

At the end of each class, the researcher will ask the teachers to purposefully mix the SEL concepts into other school curriculums and less organized times (e. g., lunch, recess, bus). Then the children were asked to work together with their parents to finish the homework about this program. Parents are encouraged to take part in this program with their children through these two years.

Mind UP: Mind UP, is a 15-class course from preschool to Grade 8 based on neuroscience, thinking consciousness, positive psychology and social emotion learning (Schonert-Reichl, Roeser & Maloney, 2016). Each class is based on the previous lesson, which transforms participants' internal into cognitive sentiments. Teachers will instruct and emphasize every component during the teaching day.

Collaborative and Proactive Solutions: Greene (2016) Collaborative and Proactive Solutions, formerly Collaborative Problem Solving (CPS) "boots settling a dispute fellowship, enable children to solve issues that impact their lives, brings more affirmative, lasting measures, while simultaneously initiating problem-solving techniques" (p. 3). The project aims to assist teachers and administrators acknowledge the inconformity between students and grown-ups. It is also designed to decrease maladjustment to harmful trauma, assuming that "kids will do well on the condition that they have the ability" and "kids will do well on the condition that they have the intention" (p. 10).

Greene is convinced that sentimental techniques could be instructed according to a mutual beneficial student and teacher interpersonal relationship (Battistich, Schaps, Watson, Solomon & Lewis, 2000; West, Day, Somers & Baroni, 2014). Stormont, Reinke, Herman and Lembke (2012) approved that this kind of social-cognitive method of learning could greatly alter students' thinking pattern. Plumb et al. (2016) explicated that this was resulted in brain nervous system development during the intervention.

Strong Kids, A Social and Emotional Learning Curriculum: The Strong Kids series include a set of course handbooks for five levels of adolescent psychological health development: (a) Strong Start (Pre-K), (b) Strong Start (Grades K to 2), (c) Strong Kids (Grades 3 to 5), (d) Strong Kids (Grades 6 to 8), and (e) Strong Teens (Grades 9 to 12) (Carrizales-Engelmann et al., 2016; Whitcomb & Parisi Damico, 2016).

Oregon University professors and their graduate students cooperated to invent the first edition of the Strong Kids series curriculum. These students took part in the Merrell's (2008) Oregon Resilience Program, because some worrying studies have shown that students' psychological health challenges have risen significantly and there were not enough resources to assist these students (Durlak et al., 2011; Greenberg et al., 2003). Merrell et al. (2008) implemented a few pilot studies for the purpose of setting up intentional interventions for students and educators.

Strong Start: *Strong Start* (Grades K to 2) is to satisfy the requirements of children aged 5 to 8 and supply the basis for the whole success of the school (Whitcomb et al. , 2016). According to the author's suggestion, the course is lectured in children's language and an amicable mascot whose name is Henry is applied during the course. Every class needs 45 minutes to finish, but it can be divided into several segments if needed.

The "Strong Kids" writers believe that effective intervention is based on successful implementation. They offered teachers with assistance by proposing active coordination, action administration, modification for different learners and resource administration, so as to develop a Strong Kids community (Whitcomb et al. , 2016). The Strong Start (Grades K to 2) course program complies with the same rules as any other Strong Kids teaching recourses, but is adjusted according to the development level of young students, and is introduced in 10 classes.

Strong Kids: Strong Kids 3 to 5 and 6 to 8 consists of 12 classes. Every class lasts 30 to 90 minutes. The course initiator encourage teachers to use handout materials more closely to satisfy the special student requirements in each class. Carrizales-Engelmann et al. (2016) offered clear and definite direction and allow adjustments owning to time limits (Running Short on Time) in the 2nd edition. The Strong Kids 2nd edition is the curriculum which was used in the current study as the original SEL intervention.

2.5.4   Strong Kids Series Studies

The prime Strong Kids pilot was implemented in a mainly White (97 percent), middle bourgeoisie (96 percent) community school with 120 liberal-education kids in Grade 5. Every lesson was lectured weekly in 5 separate classrooms, each lesson lasted 45 minutes. The assessment model of pretest and posttest was used to determine the growth of students' explicit SEL knowledge by SEL knowledge test. It evaluated the mean score differences and paired-sample t-test was used to evaluate the difference of content knowledge. The average pretest score of the students was 11.39 ($SD = 2.82$). The average posttest score of the students was 14.35 ($SD = 3.47$), identifying a great improvement ($p < 0.001$)

in SEL knowledge (Merrell et al. , 2008).

The second pilot study was conducted in the same research. It contained 65 white students (100 percent) who studied in a public junior middle school in the northwestern USA (Merrell et al. , 2008). The course applied is Strong Kids course for Grades 6 to 8. There was one lesson each week. Each lesson required 50 minutes to accomplish, and it lasted 12 weeks. Teacher's skills in learning techniques were invited to teach these lessons.

In this study, Merrell et al. (2008) included the teacher training into the research process before the implementation of the project, and provided continuous assistance as needed. They also used pretest and posttest to explore gains in SEL knowledge. The paired-sample t-test proclaimed vital gains ($p < 0.01$) in content knowledge from pretest (M = 12.46, S = 2.68) to posttest (M = 14.80, SD = 3.25), t (64) = 6.10, $p < 0.001$, resulted in a small significant effect size (0.35). Merrell et al. (2008) quoted "Remarkable and clinically relevant inprovements in SEL knowledge and reduction in passive social-sentimental symptoms" were observed in this research (p. 219).

Merrell et al. (2008) implemented the third Strong Kids study with a truly special education high school student, which included Black (75 percent) students from Grade 9 to 12. The Strong Teens (Grade 9 to 12) was utilized throughout this research. 14 students in the investigation "qualified for Individualized Education Plans (IEP) under the Emotionally Disturbed classification" (Merrell et al. , 2008, p. 219). These participants attended alternative high schools in the district because of their extreme sentiment and action requirements. In this study, a Strong Kids expert guided and cooperated with the senior school special education instructor to conduct the course.

Because of the limited sample size (N = 14) and skewed distribution, it was impossible to use paired-sample t-test for data analysis (Merrell et al. , 2010). In this case, the Wilcoxon Signed Ranks, parametric test of 2 relevant Samples was utilized to survey outcomes. Even though the sample size was quite small (N = 14), it was observed to have notable interaction effect ($p < 0.001$) between pretest $(M = 20.36, SD = 5.44)$ and posttest $(M = 22.36, SD = 4.01)$.

After a preliminary study, Merrell et al. (2008) and his research group members launched a bunch of particular projects and field-based surveys that used the course as a widespread and focus intervention (see Table 2.1).

Table 2.1

Previous Strong Kids investigations

Curriculum	Grade	Description	Empirical research
Strong start	Pre-K	10-lessons, ECE	Felver, 2013; Gunter et al., 2012;
			Howard, 2014
Strong start	K to 2	10-lessons, primary	Barker, 2015; Caldarella et al., 2009;
			Fewkes, 2017; Kramer et al., 2010;
			Kramer, 2013; Schwartz, 2016; Sicotte, 2012; Whitcomb, 2009;
Strong kids	3 to 5	12-lessons, intermediate	Bruni, 2015; Cook et al., 2015; Faust, 2006; Feuerborn, 2004; Gueldner & Feuerborn, 2016; Harlacher & Merrell, 2010; Kramer, 2013; Marchant et al., 2010; Merrell et al., 2008; Nakayama, 2008; Tran, 2007; Williams, 2015
Strong kids	6 to 8	12-lessons, intermediate	Berry-Krazmein & Torres-Fernandez, 2007; Feuerborn, 2004; Gueldner, 2007; Gueldner & Feuerborn, 2016, Levitt, 2009; Merrell et al., 2008

Note. This table was made after an extensive search of Strong Kids SEL courses in December 2017. All research used Strong Kids series (1st ed.).

Until the time for current research, the Strong Kids team has completed 32 preceding studies (Taylor, et al., 2017). Less than 50 percent of the studies were carried out by experimental designs. All studies demonstrated that students' SEL knowledge has improved according to the SEL knowledge Test. Merely three studies announced that participants reported social emotional ability and resilience increased (Harlacher & Merrell, 2010; Kramer, Caldarella, Christensen & Shatzer, 2010; Nakayama, 2008) and merely one research (Kramer, 2013) contained school participants with different demographic characteristics.

Castro-Olivo's study (2014) invited 40 Latino immigrant students to use a Strong Kids course with translated language. A more culturally appropriate adapted Strong Teens (Grades 9 to 12) course was introduced to new-immigrant students who studied in Latino senior school. This program was set up to improve new-immigrant students' scholarly and social-emotional techniques to fit to the main current USA senior school. The average SEL knowledge score improved 2. 5 point from pretest to posttest with a big effect size (ES = 0. 95). The improvement manifested that only 15 percent of these new-immigrant students had stayed in the USA for more than 24 months.

Isava (2006) conducted one research which utilized Strong Teens course. In this research, the Strong Teens course was applied as part of the psychological health guidance in 24-hour inpatient facilities. The researchers tried to explore if this course would be beneficial to the chronic social emotional and behavioral issues. Although the outcomes from pretest to posttest were not statistically significant, the score variances (M = 1. 57) across participants was significant. The rating scale of externalizing behavior between the intervention group and control group was moderate (ES = 0. 42).

Similar to Castro-Olivo's study (2014), White and Rayle (2007) adjusted the Strong Teens course to guide African American young boys in sub-committee session at a senior school. It contained special adjustment, but was not limited to the famous African American people in history and meaningful cultural norm activity.

According to Harlacher and Merrell (2010), they believed that the Strong Kids course could be utilized at school as a common implementation within a tiered system of support. Hence, they tested 106 students who studied in Grade 3 and 4 (54 percent girls, 46 percent boys). They wanted to investigate if the students would have better social-emotional abilities and have the capacity to obtain these techniques over a long period of time (Harlacher & Merrell, 2010).

Harlacher and Merrell (2010) utilized a two-way mixed effect multivariate analyses of variance with condition and time of assessment to invest social-emotional abilities. There was a significant interaction effect between the variables

$(p < 0.01)$. It also showed a significant effect on SEL knowledge from pretest to posttest $(p < 0.01)$ and even post hoc phase half a year after the accomplishment of the lessons. These outcomes contained medium effect sizes $(d = 0.73)$ among all groups.

In Kramer (2013) study, the first edition of SEL course "Strong Kids" was used as independent variable. He proposed a non-equivalent control group design in two suburban primary schools in Utah $(N = 614)$. At the treatment school $(n = 348)$, the ethnic demographic contained students from predominantly Hispanic (61 percent) and White (37 percent) communities and the demographics at the control school were similar, Hispanic (52 percent) and White (43 percent). Approximately 82 percent of students had free school lunch.

Kramer's (2013) purpose was to ascertain if the Strong Kids (1st ed.) was valid to satisfy students' need of social emotion, in addition to teachers' perceived social validity of the program. Using the school social behavior scales, they found a statistically significant interaction effect $(p < 0.001)$. The internalized and externalized behaviors of the students were ranked by two behavior rating scales. One scale is systematic screening for behavior disorders, the other scale is student risk screening scale, with the aim of validating teacher ratings of students internalizing and externalizing behaviors.

The results demonstrated that the internalization action of high-risk students greatly reduced $(p < 0.05)$. Compared with the same kind of studies, teachers' assessment of students' social techniques is relatively high (Harlacher & Merrell, 2010; Kramer et al., 2010). Better student achievement is helpful to improve social emotional capacity and active school atmosphere.

In Kramer's (2013) research, the large number of participants provided further support to make Strong Kids as a widespread course. Nevertheless, although no restrictions were referred to in the research, this study was conducted at a career development school. The teachers from this school had routine cooperation with the University. This may change the results of the study, because participants had worked with universities before and may cause a

Hawthorne effect or an observer effect and may lead to the unnatural growth of prosocial behavior. In addition, the above conclusion also provide support for Strong Kids as an efficacious widespread course.

To sum up, the literature review of SEL, especially the Strong Kids curriculum offered a lot of proof to support SEL in K-12 education (e. g., Kramer, 2013; Merrell et al., 2008; Tran, 2007; White & Rayle, 2007). Several studies have demonstrated that thanks to SEL intervention, people's comprehension of healthy patterns of showing feelings, ideas and deeds has improved, no matter what environment or grade level it is. (e. g., Merrell et al., 2008). Furthermore, it is hopeful to add Strong Kids to existing core courses at school (Gunter et al., 2012; Sicotte, 2012; Whitcomb, 2009).

2.5.5 Present SEL Intervention to Decrease Learning Anxiety and Dropout Rate in China

SEL intervention has been widely used in developed countries, such as the USA and England for a long time. However, in developing countries, SEL interventions are rarely implemented, such as in Myanmar, there is only one reported SEL intervention which applied mindfulness meditation training for adolescents whose parents were affected by HIV (Carroll et al., 2021). There is also only one reported SEL intervention which is called PATHS in Pakistan (Barlas, N. S., Sidhu, J., & Li, C., 2021).

At present, there are two reported SEL intervention in China. One is operated by Ministry of Education of China (MoE) and United Nations Children's Fund (Li et al., 2018). This official program used a curriculum adapted from the support materials provided by the learning behavioral center of Northampton University, England. This curriculum has seven lessons, including "New start" "Quarrel and reconciliation" "Say No to bullying" "Moving towards the goal" "Like myself" "Interpersonal relationship" and "Change".

This SEL intervention is delivered by class teachers and key teachers, one class per week, and every grade has different curriculum, in need of the cooperation of teachers, parents and schools. This kind of SEL intervention is time-consuming and expensive to run, and there are no report of reducing learning anxiety and dropout intention.

The other SEL intervention was implemented by Wang et al. (2016), which was specially aimed at reducing learning anxiety and dropout rates. This research used its own curriculum which was compiled by educational psychologist from Beijing Normal University. In this intervention, music, art and PE teachers were all invited to implement the curriculum. Wang et al. (2016) chose these types of teachers because they had more spare time, compared to main subject teachers. However, the effect was not strong enough. It has reduced learning anxiety only by 2.3 percent and dropout rate by 1.6 percent, while the real learning anxiety is 66 percent and the dropout rate ranges from 7.2 percent to 27.1 percent.

2.6　Teacher Autonomy Support Intervention on Students' Dropout

2.6.1　Self-determination Theory

Self-determination Theory (SDT; Deci & Ryan, 1985, 2000) is a conceptual framework for proposing distinct kinds of motivation. It also underlines the importance of meeting the three basic psychological needs (autonomy, ability and relationship), for the purpose of achieving the best private developments. From the definition of SDT, motivation is a multi-dimensional structure, indicating that distinct kinds of motivation are related to different causes of potential behavior (Deci & Ryan, 1985, 2000). In this theory, the style of incentive is more significant than the total aggregation of incentive when predicting the results (Deci & Ryan, 2008).

SDT shows that motivation varies with the persistence of self-determination. Individuals perform their behavior with complete autonomy and selection when they have more self-determined motivation. On the contrary, when individuals have less self-determined motivation, their performance are under outer constraints to achieve particular results (Deci & Ryan, 1985, 2000).

Several studies have confirmed the effectiveness of this continuity in education and other life areas (Vallerand, 1997). Internal motivation delegates the top level of self-determination. Individuals will carry out behaviors for the purpose of obtaining their inherent joy and gratification when they have intrinsic motivation (Deci & Ryan, 1985). For instance, students who have internal motivation will happily attend school to learn new knowledge. However, if individuals have external motivation, they use one activity to achieve another goal (Deci & Ryan, 1985, 2000), such as the students want to have high scores in the final examinations to get the award of a summer holiday journey with parents.

Deci and Ryan (2000) put forward distinct modalities of extrinsic regulatory manner, representing distinguished degrees of self-determination. The ways of supervision are exterior supervision, insertion supervision and identification supervision from the lowest to highest self-determination (Deci & Ryan, 1985, 2000).

The action of external regulation is demonstrated by external sources. For instance, students who are forced to go to school by guardian or law demonstrated external supervision. Introversion appears when antecede external drive source is partly internalized but not fully accepted by individuals. Students show this rule in school to avoid feeling guilty about dropping out. When an activity is determined to be of individual value and significance, a higher format of outer motivation for self-determination arises, which is called identified regulation. Students will attend school because they want to find a good job which needs profound education background to prove identified regulation.

Amotivation which happens when taking in an activity is considered to have no effect on the wanted outcome. This regulatory approach is identical with the conception of "learned helplessness" (Abramson, Seligman, & Teasdale, 1978), and is shown when the students are uncertain about the reasons for going to school. Amotivated students consider attending school is useless, or they can't anticipate the results of their actions. They usually think that their actions are brought about by outside forces that they can not control. They commonly consider their actions are caused by external forces beyond their control. Students feel powerless and are short of control when they have amotivation (Deci & Ryan, 1985). Students with amotivation used to know why they attend school, but now they are doubtful about continuing school.

2.6.2   Basic Psychological Needs

SDT believes that each individual is active in fulfiling his or her internal psychological needs: autonomy, ability and relatedness. Even though human growth spontaneously tends to be more autonomous, people must nurture their behaviors based on the experience of autonomy, ability and relatedness. According to SDT, a need is the intrinsic psychological driving force we must fulfil if we want to improve development, integrity and private happiness (Deci & Ryan, 2000).

The need for autonomy means the experience of mental freedom and will. It is the fountain of our own action (DeCharms, 1968; Deci & Ryan, 1985). Competence need means the validity and self-confidence that a person experiences in cooperation with the outside world and the social context (Deci & Ryan, 2002). Finally, the need for relatedness implies caring for others and feeling connected with others, belonging to others and communities (Deci & Ryan, 2002).

People expand and boom in circumstance conducive to fulfil three fundamental psychological requirements. The circumstance that meets these requirements is conducive to internalization and healthy mental functions, and the prevention of these needs will result in negative results. More concretely, the environment of autonomy support sustain autonomy, well-formed environmental support capabilities, and concerns and responds to the environment to promote reciprocity (Deci & Ryan, 2002; Vansteenkiste, Niemiec, & Soenens, 2010).

Briefly speaking, when individuals do not meet their fundamental mental needs, they are more likely to perform actions due to non-self-determination. Whereas if people satisfy their needs, they will perform actions due to self-determination.

Autonomous action is related to better function and perseverance and manipulated action frequently result in self-regulation issues and failures. Based on SDT, motivation plays an intermediary function in meeting basic mental needs and the resulting actions or consequences (Deci & Ryan, 1985, 2002). Therefore, from the application viewpoint, to offer students a context which can meet these three basic mental needs, teachers should improve their learning motivation. Accordingly, as time goes by, this will bring about academic persistence.

2.6.3 Teacher Autonomy Supportive Behaviors

Classroom environment has some factors that have combined action to influence students' motivation. SDT states that when students experience autonomy, they will show positive school achievements, improved ingenuity, higher comfort and endeavor, aspiring mood and motivation (Reeve & Jang, 2006).

In education context, teacher autonomy support (TAS) refers to teacher's providing students with autonomy based on classroom dynamics (Jang et al., 2010). The definition of autonomy in SDT is the origination of characteristics of TAS. Deci and Ryan (1985) proposed incidents and environment which will sustain autonomy or manipulate behavior. Under manipulated circumstances, material awards have non-positive effect on self-determination and undermine internal motivations.

In addition, in autonomy supportive activities, students are reported to be able to enhance their intrinsic motivation by offering choices, completing tasks in a way they like, and offering affirmative feedback on their abilities (Deci & Ryan, 1987). Afterwards, Reeve and his collaborators conducted numerous studies, in which TAS has become a powerful structure on schoolroom autonomy dimensionalities (Reeve & Halusic, 2009; Reeve & Jang, 2006).

These studies provide a lot of guidance on how to sustain students' autonomous learning in the schoolroom circumstance. Moreover, a few of other interposing studies have confirmed these factors of TAS in school environments (Su & Reeve, 2011). Autonomous support behaviours include listening to students' opinions carefully, providing students the chances to voice their own ideas and work in the way they like, allowing students to control teaching objects, listening to and approving their opinions, explaining reasons for required action, providing encouragement and providing commendation as rewards.

Environments which can promote teacher autonomy support have an important contribution to students' learning and academic performance in different cultures (Kaul, 2015). In school, the instructors can bring about circumstances for autonomy support based on their interpersonal relationships and motivational styles (Reeve, 2006).

2. 6. 4   Effectiveness of Teacher Autonomy Support for Intervention

Individuals can learn to support others more autonomously, which has been proved correct in the empirical research with future instructors (Barch, 2006; Reeve, 1998), primary school instructors (Collins, 2001; DeCharms, 1976), middle school physical education instructors (Chatzisarantis & Hagger, 2009; Tessier et al., 2008), high school instructors (Reeve et al., 2004), college exercise instructors (Cheon & Moon, 2010; Edmunds et al., 2008), coaches (Sullivan, 2005), physicians (Williams et al., 1999, 2002), counselors (Williams et al., 2006), medical interns (Williams & Deci 1996), and company managers (Hardré & Reeve, 2009). However, it is more efficacious to cultivate teacher to be autonomy-supportive, compared to other professions, such as medical practitioners and operational site administrative staff.

In the educational environment, when teachers support students' autonomy, students will demonstrate educational and developmental benefits, such as better participation, higher level of learning quality, preference for the best challenges, improved internal motivation, improved happiness and higher level of school record (Guay et al., 2008; Reeve et al., 2004; vansteenkister et al., 2004).

2.6.5　Teacher Autonomy Supportive Intervention on Students' Dropout

Previous studies have demonstrated that TAS fosters students' intrinsic motivation resources and assists in reducing dropout ratios. Hardre and Reeve (2003) debated elements that lead to school dropouts, such as the relationship with schoolmates and parents, and economic conditions.

However, there is a consensus that teachers cannot make a contribution to the off-campus environment to cut down dropouts, but teachers can make active contributions in the classroom environment to strengthen perseverance. If students' requirements are overlooked or thwarted, they can easily start to form the intention of dropping out. Compared to control students' interest, if teachers protect students' interest in the classroom, students will cherish their study and the possibility of discontinuing their study will be very low.

Vallerand et al. (1997) also indicated that school dropout has become an enormous social issue. The vital reason is that students have no motivation. In their research, they found that if teacher autonomy support is high, the students will have more learning perseverance, thus decreasing the discontinuing of students' studies.

In addition, Vansteenkiste et al. (2005) conducted a research revealed that students who felt under control would have higher dropout rates of their registered courses. The sense of autonomy provided them with excuse and enjoyment to seek their objectives, so the rate of drop out reduced. Consequently, teachers' autonomous support was contributed to cut down dropout rate. It was essential to require teachers to teach in the way of teachers' autonomous support.

2.7   The Limitation of Current SEL Intervention in Reducing Learning Anxiety and Dropout in China

The weak SEL intervention effect of Wang et al. (2016) may result from several reasons. Firstly, the curriculum is not evidence-based, which has not been implemented before. A school-wide, Tier I, SEL curricular tool, such as *Strong Kids* (2nd ed.) can be a good choice for reducing junior middle school students' learning anxiety and dropout rate, as it has been proven to be an evidence-based, cost-effective curriculum which can promote students' psychological health and resilience by developing health competence techniques (Merrell, Carrizales, Feuerborn, Gueldner & Tran, 2007, Hetrick, 2018).

Secondly, the types of teachers who implement the intervention may also affect the effect. Although Durlak et al. (2011) has revealed that school teachers are competent to implement the SEL curriculum, which type of school teacher is better for implementaion has not been mentioned. There are many kinds of school teachers who have been invited to implement SEL so far, such as art teacher, music teacher, PE teacher and class teacher, even principals (Merrell et. al, 2010; Wang et. al,2016).

As SEL intervention is a kind of psychological health intervention in school, psychology teachers with educational psychology background may be more familiar with the knowledge and techniques in implementing SEL, compared to other kinds of school teachers who are not majored in psychology and lacking experience in delivering psychological activities (Li, 2017).

Thirdly, how teachers deliver SEL intervention may also affect the result. Hetrick (2018) found that SEL intervention needs modification to improve student engagement and improve expected results. According to the interview to teachers who delivered SEL intervention, some teachers thought SEL intervention such as Strong Kids intervention forces students to develop a sense of community and inclusiveness. The teacher directed too much of the lesson. There is not enough student involvement. As a result, it is necessary to give students more autonomy in class to improve student's engagement, which can help to reduce students' learning anxiety and dropout.

Reeve (2010) found that teacher autonomy support can set a warm and democratic environment for students to learn. Reeve (2006) identified that there are eleven teacher autonomy support instruction behaviors, such as "asking what students want" "giving students time to work in their personal way" "giving praise feedback" "providing rationales" "giving encouragement" "giving hints", etc.

Harlacher and Merrell (2010) have found that praise and precorrection is effective to improve Pacific Northwest primary pupils' SEL knowledge and use of SEL techniques. Praise is a kind of teacher autonomy support instruction style. Harlacher and Merrell (2014) gave a clue and evidence to imply teacher's autonomy support in delivering SEL intervention.

Reeve (1998) found teacher autonomy support is teachable. Furthermore, Cheon and Reeve (2018) gave details on how to train teachers to teach in a teacher autonomy support way by the Autonomy Support Intervention Program (ASIP). However, it has not yet systematically to train teachers how to deliver SEL intervention in a teacher autonomy support way. As a result, in this research, teacher autonomy supportive instruction behaviors were added to original Strong Kids curriculum to develop TASSEL intervention.

2.8　The Significance and Development of TASSEL Intervention

Based on the weak intervention effect of existing SEL intervention in China, it is necessary to develop a more effective SEL intervention to reduce students' learning anxiety and dropout. As Strong Kids is an evidence-based and cost-effective SEL intervention, and teacher autonomy support instructions can help to improve students' engagement in SEL intervention. As a result, we applied Strong Kids intervention as our original SEL intervention model, and modified it with teacher autonomy supportive instructions. In this way, we developed our own teacher autonomy supportive social and emotional learning intervention, which is called TASSEL intervention.

Teacher Autonomy Supportive Social and Emotional Learning intervention (TASSEL) is based on emotional intelligence theory and self-determination theory, which is an enhanced SEL intervention. SEL intervention is grounded in emotional intelligence theory, especially Goleman's mixed models of EI (Goleman et al. , 2000). This mixed EI model considers emotional intelligence as a pack of sentimental and social abilities consisting of cognitive ability and personality. There are five abilities in social and emotional learning: self-awareness, self-management, social awareness, relationship management and responsible decision-making.

As SEL intervention needs modification to improve student engagement and improve expected results (Hetrick, 2018), and teacher autonomy support instructions are proven to be effective to improve student engagement and enhance expected results (Reeve, 2010). Hence, teacher autonomy support instructions were added to original SEL intervention to produce a new intervention, which is called TASSEL.

Based on Chinese culture and the pilot experiment of this study, we found that six teacher autonomy supportive instruction behaviors are suitable for Chinese students, including "allow students to choose seats and sit with their friends" "give structure about each lesson" "ask students to share their own experiments and accept students' negative emotions" "ask students to draw or write about their feeling" "give rationality and appraise on activities according to the lesson", and "allow group discussion with teamwork". Therefore, we added these six teacher autonomy supportive instructions to original SEL, and invented TASSEL intervention, the procedure of developing TASSEL intervention and the difference between TASSEL and SEL were explained in 3. 5. 1 and 3. 5. 2.

2. 9　Summary

This chapter illustrated the literature review of present study. First of all, it set up the background of this research, the high dropout rate of rural junior middle school students in China, and then it explained the reasons for students to drop out, the reasons include boarding school merger policy, the demographic reasons and the economical poverty. Meanwhile, there were also psychological reasons for students to dropout such as psychological health problem, especially learning anxiety, which was the vital psychological reason for students to dropout.

Even though it was difficult and sometimes impossible to change the external causes of student mental health problems, there were also some easy and cost-save way to change internal causes of learning anxiety and dropout. Therefore, this research concentrated on Multi-tiered Systems of Support (MTSS) to psychological health as a Tier I prevention and intervention for students with learning anxiety and dropout intention. There were many Social and Emotional Learning (SEL) Programs could be used as Tier I intervention. Compared to other curriculums, Strong Kids was an evidence-proven, cost-effective curriculum which was chosen for this research, and also there was some modification based on existing implementation of Strong Kids. We analyzed the significance of TASSEL intervention, and we wanted to develop our TASSEL intervention based on Chinese collectivism culture.

Furthermore, in this research, two factors were added to investigate TASSEL intervention effect on rural junior middle school students' psychological health, especially SEL knowledge, learning anxiety and dropout intention. One factor is teacher type. Psychology teacher was compared to regular teacher. The other factor is intervention type. TASSEL intervention was compared to original SEL intervention.

In this way, we produced four intervention groups. They were SEL intervention implemented by regular teacher (RT + SEL, group 1), teacher autonomy supportive SEL intervention implemented by regular teacher (RT + TASSEL, group 2), SEL intervention implemented by psychology teacher (PT + SEL, group 3), and teacher autonomy supportive SEL intervention implemented by psychology teacher (PT + TASSEL, group 4). According to our hypothesis, teacher autonomy supportive SEL intervention implemented by psychology teacher should have the best intervention effect on rural junior middle school students' SEL knowledge, learning anxiety and dropout intention.

CHAPTER THREE
METHODOLOGY

3. 1　Introduction

This chapter introduced the research methodology in the present study which was aimed to examine the effectiveness of the SEL intervention based on different teachers and intervention types among rural junior middle school students' SEL knowledge, learning anxiety and dropout intention. Furthermore, it also discussed the research design, validity threats of quasi-experimental design, population and sampling, intervention programs, instruments, procedures, data collection and data analysis and pilot study.

3. 2　Research Design

Quantitative methodological approaches solve a problem by measuring variables for individual respondents to acquire the data that is in the numerical form typically, and the findings are mainly the product of statistical analysis and summary (Gravetter & Forzano, 2012; Shaughnessy, Zechmeister & Zechmeister, 2012). Creswell (2012) argued that quantitative research was "particular and limited focal point, focusing on impersonal, measurable variables, and permitting for impersonal and unprejudiced methods" (p. 13).

The design of the experiment is a plan to allocate the experimental cell to the treatment level and to analyze the statistical data related to the experiment (Kirk, 1995). The experimental design confirms independent, dependent and disturbance variables, and points out random and statistical methods for conducting the experiment. The major objective of the experimental design is to establish a causal relationship between independent and dependent variables.

The second goal is to extract the maximum amount of information with the least expenditure on resources. An experimental design usually includes comparisons of two or more groups. The intervention group is named experimental group, and the group without intervention is named control group (Gay & Airasian, 2003). The most important work of experimental study is the independent variable manipulation. Control means to remove external and internal factors which might interfere with the dependent variable in the experiment. Threats control is also very important in experimental study.

Factorial design is a common experimental design in the social sciences. It can test two or more different independent variables' effects at once. Factorial design allows scholars to investigate main effects (the effects of a single variable) and potential moderators and mediators of these effects (Keppel et al., 2004). Therefore, social scientists who are mainly interested in theoretical testing often rely heavily on factorial design. The simplest factorial design is a 2 × 2 (read as a "two by two") design. In this design, two variables are operated at two different levels to produce four treatment units.

In the present research, a 2 × 2 qusai-factorial design with pretest and posttest (see Table 3.1) is used to investigate the effects of teacher type and intervention type based on Strong Kids curriculum intervention among rural junior middle school students' SEL knowledge, learning anxiety and dropout intention in rural southwest of China. A 2 × 2 quasi-factorial design with pretest and posttest was helpful to confirm the effect of teacher types and intervention types between groups before and after treatment (Keppel et al., 2004).

Table 3. 1

2 × 2 Qusai-factorial design

Teacher types	Intervention type	
	SEL	TASSEL
regular teacher（RT）	RT + SEL 1	RT + TASSEL 2
psychology teacher（PT）	PT + SEL 3	PT + TASSEL 4

SEL: Social and Emotional Learning; TASSEL: Teacher Autonomy Supportive Social and Emotional Learning.

From Table 3.1, we can see that this study is a 2 × 2 qusai-factorial design. The first 2 means two types of teacher. One type is Psychology Teacher (PT), and the other type is Regular Teacher (RT). The second 2 means two intervention types. One intervention type is Teacher Autonomy Supportive Social and Emotional Learning (TASSEL), the other intervention type is Social and Emotional Learning (SEL).

The study is a quasi-experiment because there were no real randomized participants in each case. Quasi-experiment is an approximation of experiment or "near experiment" (Sansone, Morf & Panter, 2004), which is often used in schools because of the limitation of real random assignment. Similar to randomized trials, quasi-experiments supply a useful estimate of the impact of one or more treatments on one or more variable outcomes. This study used between subjects and within subjects elements in the design. (see Table 3. 2)

Table 3. 2

Between-subjects and within-subjects pretest and posttest experimental design

	Groups	Within subjects		
		Time 1		Time 2
		Pretest	Intervention	Posttest
Between subjects	Treatment group 1（RT + SEL）	O1	X1	O2
	Treatment group 2（RT + TASSEL）	O1	X2	O2
	Treatment group 3（PT + SEL）	O1	X3	O2
	Treatment group 3（PT + TASSEL）	O1	X4	O2

From Table 3. 1 and Table 3. 2, we can see that with a 2 × 2 quasi-factorial design, there are four intervention groups in present study, and when each group has pretest and posttest, makes 8 groups compare the intervention effect between subjects and within subjects.

These four intervention groups are as follows: SEL intervention implemented by regular teacher (RT + SEL, group 1), teacher autonomy supportive SEL intervention implemented by regular teacher (RT + TASSEL, group 2), SEL intervention implemented by psychology teacher (PT + SEL, group 3), and teacher autonomy supportive SEL intervention implemented by psychology teacher (PT + TASSEL, group 4).

We randomly assigned the four intervention groups to each intervention. Among the four intervention groups, we wanted to find which one was the best combination of intervention type and teacher type to improve SEL knowledge, reduce learning anxiety and reduce dropout intention.

In a related study, Edmonds and Kennedy (2016) asserted that the pre-posttest experimental design normally assists researchers in comprehending the participants prior to the application of treatment. This also assists in making a comparison of each group's understanding after the treatment. Hence, the evaluation and assessment of the various participants' respond to the program and how it affects them are made possible.

3. 3   Validity Threats of Quasi-experimental Design

In order to strengthen the power of the experiment, it is necessary to investigate and control internal and exterior validity threats to any experimental design. Internal validity threat refers to a question such as, is the difference observed on independent variable which is caused by the treatment or other factors like extraneous variables? Similarly, external validity refers to question such as would the same difference on independent variables be observed with other subjects, other settings and at other times? The section below discussed the validity threats and control measures taken to control these threats in the present study.

3.3.1 Factors Affecting Internal Validity

Since lack of control, non-randomization is the weakness of quasi-experimental design over true experimental design. It is vital to analyze the extraneous elements that could result in alternative interpretation of results. Factors relevant to present study that can jeopardize the internal effectiveness of quasi-experimental design as follows (see Table 3.3).

Table 3.3

Internal validity threats of Quasi-experimental design

Internal validity threats	Description
Maturation	It refers to biological and physical changes that can affect the dependent variable during one of the tests such as age.
History	Other events or conditions, other than treatment that can occur between pretest and posttest and may affect dependent variable.
Pretesting	It refers to the familiarization with test instrument during pretest then is likely to affect the response on posttest.
Instrumentation	It refers to the change, such as type of instrument, difficult level, the way of test administration, the scorers, different observers.
Selection bias	It refers to the fact that it has manifest distinctions between the intervention group and the control group before the start of the experiment.
Experimental mortality	It happens when participants are lost during the experiment.
Selection-maturation interaction effect	Subjects in two different groups have different maturation rates.
Experimenter effect	It refers to the unintentional influence of experiments on the research.
Subject effects	It refers to "just the knowledge" they are participating in a study or novelty effect that can affect dependent variable.

Continued   table

Internal validity threats	Description
Diffusion	It occurs when participants in two groups interact about the treatment with each other.

3. 3. 2   Internal Validity Threats Control for the Current Study

In order to have a robust design, several precautionary measures were taken for the current study to minimize the function of those threats in a natural and causal way. The researcher was aware of preserving the essence of quasi-experimental design by not artificially controlling the regular, natural setting of learning environment. However, the following points explain the role of these threats in the current study.

3. 3. 2. 1   Maturation

Maturation refers to biological and physical changes that can affect dependent variable during one of the tests such as age. This intervention lasted for 12 weeks; it was very unlikely for students to have manifest changes both biologically and mentally to affect the results.

3. 3. 2. 2   History

History refers to other events or condition, other than treatment that can occur between pretest and posttest and may affect dependent variable. In this research, the students' response was based on Strong Kids intervention or teacher autonomy supportive Strong Kids intervention. Other social and emotional learning intervention such as PATHS would affect the result, and activities like watching SEL movies and attend other activities referring to SEL would also affect the result. In the current study, all the participants were not involved in these activities.

3.3.2.3 Pretesting

Pretesting refers to the familiarization with test instrument during pretest then is likely to affect the response on posttest. In this research, there was a 12-week time interval between pretest and posttest. The students could not remember all of the questionnaire clearly, so they were not familiar with the feedback test instrument (Brown, G., Irving, S., & Keegan, P., 2008).

3.3.2.4 Instrumentation

Instruments refers to the change of instruments, such as changing of type of instruments, difficult level, the way of test administration, the scorers. In this research, instruments were the same for pretest and posttest.

3.3.2.5 Selection Bias

Selection bias refers to the significant difference between the participants in different intervention groups even before the beginning of the experiment. In this research, all the demographic characteristics of students in each group were homogenous, including the quantity of students, gender, age and socioeconomic condition, race, and the qualifications of parents, which avoided the selection bias.

3.3.2.6 Experimental Mortality

Experimental mortality happens when participants are lost during the experiment. In the present research, all the participants were boarding school students who studied in the same school, unless there were some special occasions, such as students' serious illness, students were at school and attended all the intervention lessons.

3.3.2.7 Selection-Maturation Interaction Effect

Selection-maturity interaction effect means different groups of subjects have different maturity rates. If students with faster maturity are "selected" into one experimental group, the excellent performance of this experimental group may due to the selection-maturity rather than experimental treatment. In this study, the students in each class had the similar maturation, as they were randomly assigned to each class at the first year of junior middle school, and they were at similar age when they registered for junior middle school.

3.3.2.8   Experimenter Effect

Experimenter effect refers to inadvertently impact that the experimenter has on the research. Experimenter's individual characteristics, for instance, gender, race, age, and position, expectation and personal preference in one method over another, can affect the performance of subjects. The best approach to reduce experimenters' effectiveness is to normalize each procedure, or to have other trained people (rather than researchers) work straightly with the participators. In this study, four homogenous teachers were invited to deliver the interventions. All of the teachers were female, with a bachelor's degree, aged from 25 to 26, with 2 years' teaching experience and had no bias on any intervention types. There was also one rater who was the vice-principal of the intervention school.

3.3.2.9   Subjects Effects

Subjects Effects refer to "just the knowledge" they are participating in a study or are being observed that can affect dependent variable. In this research, for the sake of avoiding subjects effect threat, both the student participants and teacher participants were not allowed to know the objectives of this research and they were only told that they would have regular psychological well-being curriculum as usual.

3.3.2.10   Diffusion

The diffusion of treatment information from subjects in the intervention groups may affect each other. In this research, if teachers and students in one group shared information about methods and materials with teachers and students in another group, it would induce diffusion and affect the result.

In order to lessen the threat of diffusion, it was necessary to deemphasize the fact about experiment and avoid situations where students and teachers of each group could interact such as school activities, break time library activity. In this research, the researcher did not permit students to discuss the intervention and ask their teachers to tell them what shared in class should keep in class.

3.3.3　Elements Affecting External Validity

Similar to inward availability menaces, it is vital to analyse and control latent outside availability menaces to increase outcomes generalizability. The following table introduced the outside validity threats (see Table 3.4).

Table 3.4

External validity threat

External validity threats	Description
Selection-treatment interaction effects	Subjects are not selected randomly, which limits generalizability.
Setting treatment interaction effects	Artificiality or uniqueness of experimental settings limits generalizability.
Operational definition	Operational definitions of variables influence the generalizability of results.

3.3.4　External Validity Threats Control for the Present Study

The table above presents the external validity threats relevant to present study. Similar to internal validity threats, external validity threats that are more focused on generalizability issue, which is a concern for quasi-experiment designs.

3.3.4.1　Selection-Treatment Interaction Effect

Selection-treatment interaction effect refers to subjects that are not selected randomly, which limits generalizability. A major threat to the external effectiveness of the experiment is the possibility of interaction effect between participant characteristics and treatment, so the results found by certain types of individuals may not be applicable to different individuals. This interaction effect occurs when participants in a study do not represent a larger group that the researcher may want to generalize.

In this study, in order to avoid selection-treatment interaction effect, probability sampling method was used to choose a sample of rural junior middle schools in Qinzhou City, which had the homogeneous characteristics of students in the objective population and was the proper representative of the larger population to generalize.

3. 3. 4. 2   Setting-treatment Interaction Effect

Setting-treatment interaction effect refers to artificiality or uniqueness of experimental settings which may limit generalizability. Artificiality in the setting may limit the generalizability of the results. Artificial laboratory results may differ from those obtained in natural environments. In this study, it used quasi-experiment, instead of true experiment, and this study was implemented in real classroom in rural junior middle school to prevent the threat of setting treatment interaction effect. Furthermore, while this experiment was conducted in the same school, the noise, the brightness, the temperature, the general decoration of each classroom, and the class time for each class and time schedule for each week were homogenous.

3. 3. 4. 3   Operational Definition

Operational definition refers to the independent and dependent variables which influence the generalizability of results. In this study, all the operational definitions were used according to relevant theories, and were consistent between pretest and posttest. All the participants had both pretest and posttest to avoid pretest treatment interaction effect.

3. 4   Population and Sampling

3. 4. 1   Population

Population refers to the identifiable group of individuals or other units that researchers want to study their specific problems (Goodwin, 2010). As elaborated by Gravetter and Forzano (2012), a target population is a defined group of individuals based on specific interests of the researcher. Typically, those people in the target population holding similar characteristics which the investigator can identify and study.

Rural junior middle school students are the students who study in rural junior middle school from Grades 7 to 9, at the age of 13 − 15. In the present study, the target population of this research are the rural junior middle school students in Qinzhou City, Guangxi Zhuang Autonomous Region, Southwest of China. Qinzhou City, is one of the poorest places in the country, with a high dropout rate in rural junior middle schools (Li, et al. , 2013). There were 200 rural junior middle schools in this city then.

3. 4. 2   Sampling Techniques

Sampling is the procedure of the selection and identification an adequate number of elements from the population to form the sample that are able to represent the target population (Shaughnessy et al. , 2012). In quantitative approach, it is likely to generalize the results to the entire target population if the sample under study is selected carefully using the accurate sampling technique (Dawson, 2007). To obtain a sample that is representative of the rural junior middle school students' population in southwest of China, probability sampling was used in the current study, especially simple random technique.

3. 4. 2. 1   Student Participants

Rural junior middle school students are the students who study in rural junior middle school from Grades 7 to 9, at the age of 13 – 15. Previous studies have revealed that many demographic variables affect school dropout. Several studies revealed that students at the age older than 14 years old, Grade 8, live in boarding school, have poor academic achievement, with more siblings, father with less education and low family income. With all of these demographic characteristics, students will have more chances to drop out (Yi et al., 2012; Li, Zang & An, 2013; Wang et al., 2015).

In this research, the target population of this research are the rural junior middle school students in Qinzhou City, Guangxi Zhuang Autonomous Region, Southwest of China. Qinzhou is a small city in Guangxi. Poverty of culture caused junior middle school students to drop out (Bichao, H., 2005). The gross enrollment rate in high schools is only 53. 6% (Zhu, H., & Hou, L., 2020). From the Qinzhou government website, we know that the population of Qinzhou City was 4, 176, 600 in 2019. From Qinzhou Education Bureau officer, we got the data that the number of boarding school students was 140, 707 in 2019. There were 200 rural junior middle schools in the area then.

This study applied simple random sampling to select the intervention school. There are 200 rural junior middle schools, which are homogenous. The researcher got the list of these school names from the Education Bureau in Qinzhou City, and randomly chose one of the rural junior middle school to be the intervention school. In this way, Qingtang Second Junior Middle School in Qinbei District of Qinzhou City was randomly chosen to be the intervention school. In Qingtang Second Junior Middle School, there are seven classes in Grade 8. We randomly chose four classes as our intervention classes, and randomly allocated them to the intervention groups. Based on this method, a total of 209 students (107 boys, 102 girls) from four classes in Grade 8 were selected to take part in the experiment. The student participants' average age was 14. 3 years old. See Table 3. 5.

Table 3. 5

Participating student demographics

Demographics	Group 1	Group 2	Group 3	Group 4	Total
Male	29	20	32	26	107
Female	22	30	23	27	102
Total	51	50	55	53	209
Grade 8 boarding	Grade 8 boarding	Grade 8 boarding	Grade 8 boarding	Grade 8 boarding	Grade 8 boarding

3. 4. 2. 2   Teacher Participants

Experimental effect is a vital effect of internal validity. Hence, it is critical to be aware of how to choose teachers to implement the intervention. First of all, it is vital to make sure all the variables of the selected teachers are matched except different methodology and education background. In this research, the teachers have the same gender; all are females, similar age of 25 – 26, with 2 years' teaching experience, 11 – 13 hours per week and similar monthly salary, 1585 – 1695 *yuan* per month. Table 3. 6 showed the demographic information of teachers who took part in this study.

Table 3. 6

Participating teachers demographics

Items	Teacher A	Teacher B	Teacher C	Teacher D
Gender	Female	Female	Female	Female
Age	26	26	25	25
Qualification	Bachelor in psychology	Bachelor in psychology	Bachelor in Chinese	Bachelor in Chinese
Working years	2 years	2 years	2 years	2 years
Teaching hours/week	13 hours	12 hours	11 hours	12 hours
Monthly salary (*yuan*)	1695 *yuan*	1676 *yuan*	1585 *yuan*	1659 *yuan*

Matching teachers on all variables except methodology: The rural junior middle school chosen for the present experiment had seven classes in Grade 8. Therefore, there are seven teachers who teach students psychological well-being classes. There are only two psychology teachers who have two classes, so there are five Chinese teachers to teach psychological well-being class. In order to eliminate experimental effect, it was recommended to have almost identical teacher (Gall et al. , 2002). In this research, we focused on comparing the teacher type (psychology teacher VS regular teacher) in our intervention, and all other demographic characteristics like different age, working year, teaching hour per week, and salary should be identical. In this way, three teachers who were much older than the other four teachers were eliminated from the study. The other four left teachers were equalized on all variables except for teacher type.

3. 4. 2. 3   Teachers Assignment for Intervention Groups

Furthermore, in order to compare the effect of TASSEL versus original SEL, it is necessary to ascertain that the different effect is resulted in different intervention type only (teacher autonomy support or not), but not because of other characteristics of the teachers. Reeve (1998) has identified that teacher motivating style has three influence factors, such as personality, interpersonal style and motivating style. The General Causality Orientation Scale (GCOS), which ranges from autonomy supportive to control or impersonal, was applied to assess the motivating style of teachers, and used to select teachers for intervention group in this study.

General Causality Orientation Scale (GCOS): Teachers are very important in treatment procedure because they are responsible to induce treatment and manipulate independent variable among participants of treatment groups. Reeve et al. (2004) discovered that trained teachers demonstrated significantly more autonomy supportive actions than did untrained or delayed training group teachers. In another study, Reeve (1998) concluded that self-determination theory identified three sources that influenced teachers' motivating styles. First, it's a matter of personality. Second, it is a way of interpersonal communication which is made up of acquired techniques. Third, motivating styles that varies according to social contexts.

Self-determination theory also explains the factors that energies individual teacher behaviours as "causality orientation", to undertake tasks such as teaching. If an individual indulges in a behavior for interest reasons, then an autonomy causality orientation is considered the cause of their behaviours. Therefore, it is considered appropriate to select and train teachers to participate in autonomy supportive training.

Consistent with Reeve (1998), four chosen teachers were assessed for their causality orientation for autonomy using General Causality Orientation Scale (GCOS) in the present study. The personality orientation is that scale ranges from autonomy supportive to control or impersonal. Teachers who scored more than 60 for autonomy were selected for Teacher Autonomy Support Social and Emotional Learning (TASSEL) training, and the other teachers were selected for Social and Emotional Learning (SEL) training, as demonstrated in Table 3.7.

Table 3.7

Selection of teachers for each intervention group

Teacher type		Autonomy	Control	Impersonal	Selection for intervention group
Psychology teacher	Teacher A	61	53	38	TASSEL group
	Teacher B	57	47	41	SEL group
Regular teacher	Teacher C	63	49	46	TASSEL group
	Teacher D	44	45	35	SEL group

From Table 3.7, we can see that for psychology teachers, teacher A was chosen as TASSEL group intervention teacher, as teacher A got a higher score on autonomy than the other psychology teacher (teacher B). Teacher B was selected as SEL group intervention teacher. For regular teachers, Teacher C was chosen as TASSEL group intervention teacher, as she got higher score on autonomy than the other regular teacher (teacher D), and teacher D was selected as SEL group intervention teacher.

3. 5   Intervention Programs

In this research, there were two kinds of interventions. One was original Strong Kids curriculum intervention, the other one was teacher autonomy support Strong Kids curriculum intervention.

3. 5. 1   SEL Intervention Program

Strong Kids (2nd version) (Carrizales-Engelmann et al. , 2016) in Grades 6 – 8 is a structural intervention course with the purpose of instructing social and emotional techniques and enhancing coping techniques. This course is based on excellent practices in present social and emotional development research and social techniques training literature. The course concepts focus on five social and emotional techniques described by Cowen (1994), including self-awareness, self-management, social awareness, relationship techniques and responsible decision-making. The course focuses on solving internal problems and improving resilience (Merrell et al. , 2007). This course can teach the techniques through clear instruction in an easy-to-use form.

According to Carrizales-Engelmann et al. (2016), Strong Kids Grades 6 – 8 includes 12 weekly lessons. Each lesson takes about 45 minutes. The course includes the following parts: technique introduction, technique modeling, application activities and teamwork. Each class also includes "Transfer Training Techniques", which aims to extend techniques to other settings and maintain skills over time. The course begins with a review of the techniques previously taught. Strong Kids' classes are carefully arranged. Lessons learned are shown in Table 3. 8, and there is a sample lesson in Appendix A (see Appendix A).

Table 3. 8

Strong Kids lessons

Lesson	Content
Lesson 1 About Strong Kids: emotional strength training	Overview of the course, participation expectations, and key words
Lesson 2 Understanding your feelings 1	Discriminate basic feelings and comprehend how feelings are comfortable or uncomfortable
Lesson 3 Understanding your feelings 2	Identify appropriate ways of expressing feelings
Lesson 4 Understanding other people's feelings	use physical cues to identify others' emotions
Lesson 5 Dealing with anger	Identify anger and ways to control anger
Lesson 6 Clear thinking 1	Comprehend the effect of thinking on feelings and actions, inward thinking awareness, and common thought gists that influence action, ideas and sentiments
Lesson 7 Clear thinking 2	Foster the capacity to pay attention to or observe ideas, distinguish healthy and less helpful modes
Lesson 8 Solving people's problems	Learn how to understand your behavior while keeping a good manner, differentiate between serviceable and unserviceable decision strategies, and discern and use problem-solving procedures to handle conflicts
Lesson 9 Letting go of stress	Comprehend variety types of proactively stress coping methods
Lesson 10 Positive living	Comprehend the value of vigorous options
Lesson 11 Creating strong and smart goals	Set goals and increase active activities as a healthy lifestyle
Lesson 12 Finishing up	Review concepts and techniques about the course

Note. Adapted from Carrizales-Engelmann et al. , 2016.

3. 5. 2　TASSEL Intervention Program

In order to develop TASSEL intervention, we took the following four steps to compile it. First, we discussed with Chinese psychologists and junior middle school psychology teachers about which teacher autonomy supportive instructions should be added to the original SEL intervention. After discussion, we agreed with five instructions, including "give structure about each lesson" "ask students to share their own experiments and accept students' negative emotions" "ask students to draw or write about their feelings" "give rationality and appraise on activities according to the lesson", and "allow group discussion with teamwork".

The second step was to have a two-week pilot experiment to check our TASSEL intervention. We invited two psychological teachers in another junior middle school to implement the TASSEL intervention every day, and the researcher went to their classes every day to observe, and found that the original warm-up activity was not workable for these students, so we added one more teacher autonomy supportive instruction which was called "warm-up activities chosen by students". In this way, we had six teacher autonomy supportive instructions. The third step was that we found that some keywords were difficult for Chinese students to understand, so we modified it based on Chinese culture to help students better understand the keywords. The last step was that we showed our modified version of TASSEL intervention to psychological experts and junior middle school psychology teachers again to get more suggestion to modify it, and then after revision, we got our final version of TASSEL intervention.

The primary differences between SEL and TASSEL were the delivery and instructional techniques to implement the intervention, based on original SEL intervention, Chinese culture and our pilot experiment. Six additional TAS instructions were chosen to be added to the original SEL intervention, including "warm-up activities chosen by students" "give structure about each lesson" "ask students to share their own experiments and accept students' negative emotions" "ask students to draw or write about their feeling" "give rationality and appraise on activities according to the lesson", and "allow group discussion with teamwork". Additionally, several activities in the original SEL were not culturally appropriate, thus the new intervention comprised counselling activities that were aligned with the Chinese culture. The comparison between TASSEL intervention and SEL intervention was shown in Table 3.9. The TASSEL intervention lesson outlines were shown in Appendix B.

Table 3. 9

Teacher autonomy support Strong Kids VS original Strong Kids lesson

Minutes	TASSEL intervention	SEL intervention
0 – 3	Warm-up activities chosen by students	Review of last lesson
4 – 6	Review last lesson	Introduce the goal of new lesson
7 – 8	Introduce the structure and goal of new lesson	Mindfulness-based focusing activity
9 – 13	Key terms and definitions (explain according to Chinese culture, use examples based on students' own experience)	Key terms and definitions
14 – 32	Activities according to each lesson (Give rational and appraise on activities according to the lesson)	Activities according to each lesson
33 – 38	Group work for teamwork	Putting it all together & Closure
39 – 42	Free talk time (leisure time between students and teacher)	Tips for transfer training and teamwork
43 – 45	Putting it all together & Closure	Teamwork handout (personal)

3. 6 Instruments

There are five questionnaires used in present study. Three questionnaires are applied as dependent variables, including SEL knowledge test, learning anxiety index and dropout intention. There are also another two surveys. One is for teacher chosen survey, which is called General Causality Orientation Scale (GCOS). We used this survey to select and allocate teachers to TASSEL intervention or SEL intervention, based on their special score on autonomy as discussed in teacher selection part. The other questionnaire is used for teacher autonomy fidelity check. The survey is called Learning Climate Questionnaire

(LCQ). We used this survey to check if teachers provide teacher autonomy supportive behaviors in their class during the intervention procedures.

In this study, the questionnaires which were selected to study the effect of intervention have been widely used in SEL series of studies. Except learning anxiety which has been used in Chinese culture, SEL knowledge and dropout intention survey were the first time to be used in China. When used in different cultures, it is essential to check the effectiveness and reliability of instruments (Triandis, 1976; Grunert & scherhorn, 1990). The instruments used in this study were translated into Chinese by back translation (Brislin, 1970). We invited a Chinese lecturer from Guizhou University. She was a local Chinese, and she obtained her Ph. D. in psychology in England. Then we invited another Chinese lecturer from educational psychology background to translate Chinese into English. Then, we compared the translated English version with the original one to ensure that they have the same meaning. After back-to-back translation, we conducted a pilot study to test internal consistency, using Cronbach's alpha internal consistency reliability test. The summary of the instruments in present study is shown in Table 3. 10.

Table 3. 10

Summary of the instruments in present study

Participants	Purpose of instruments	Name of instruments	Number of items	Range
Students	Dependent variable 1	Strong Kids knowledge	20	0 − 20
Students	Dependent variable 2	Learning anxiety	15	0 − 15
Students	Dependent variable 3	Dropout intention	3	1 − 6
Teachers	Teacher selection	General Causality Orientation Scale (GCOS)	12	1 − 6
Students	Teacher autonomy supportive behavior fidelity check	Learning Climate Questionnaire (LCQ)	6	1 − 6

3.6.1 SEL Knowledge

SEL Knowledge Questionnaire. The 20 items self-report knowledge questionnaire was designed to be used to assess the knowledge of healthy social emotional and behavioral techniques before and after the test, especially the concepts taught in the Strong Kids Course (see Appendix C). Knowledge questionnaire is essentially a way to measure students' knowledge, especially social and emotional coping strategies and knowledge, by relating the content taught in the course.

These items consist of true and false items and multiple selection items. Each item is scored correctly or incorrectly by using the scoring keys provided in the course. Correct answer gets 1 point for each question, correct completion of all test questions up to 20 points. The final correct score can be converted to the percentage of correct answers. Examples include: marking right or wrong— "Self-esteem is your sense of value to yourself", multiple choices— "An example of uncomfortable emotions for most people is (a) excitement, (b) frustration, (c) curiosity, (d) content".

The SEL Knowledge Questionnaire has been used in several pilot studies (Feuerborn, 2004; Faust, 2006; Isava, 2006). Previous studies have shown that these 20 measures are sensitive to changes in knowledge among students participating in the project. Internal consistency reliability (Cronbach's alpha) ranges from 0.60 to 0.70, which is considered sufficient for a research measurement of this length.

3.6.2 Learning Anxiety

The study used a variant of the children's dominant anxiety scale, known as the Learning Anxiety Index (Reynolds & Richmond, 1978) (see Appendix D). The Learning Anxiety Index (LA) is the most widely used scale to measure the anxiety of junior middle school students in China (Yao et al., 2011; Zhou,

1991). It consists of 15 questions raised by the Mental Health Test (MHT) (Gan, Bi & Ruan, 2007; Zhou, 1991). Each item uses a yes or no answer. Correct answer gets 1 point for each question, correct completion of all test questions up to 15 points. More than 8 points on this variable implies higher levels of learning anxiety, less than 3 indicates low level of learning anxiety (Yao et al., 2011). The reliability of LA ranges from 0.84 to 0.88, and that of retest ranges from 0.78 to 0.86 (Yao et al., 2011).

3.6.3 Dropout Intention

Intentions to persist versus drop out test. This scale was used to test rural junior middle school students' intention to drop out. It includes two items to assess the willingness to stick to school or drop out. From Vallerand et al. (1997), sample items are "I sometimes think about dropping out" and "I intend to drop out". Each item uses a six-point Likert-type scale ranging from 1 (strongly disagreed) to 6 (strongly agreed). In the Vallerand et al. (1997) survey, the two items are highly correlated with each other. One year later, the questionnaire predicts actual dropout behavior and is sensitive to students' motivation. A third inquiry about continuing education intention was added to the questionnaire (see Appendix E). "Sometimes I feel uncertain about continuing to study year after year." A score more than 9 means students have dropout intention. The scale has been shown to be reliable, with Cronbach's alpha of about 0.78 (Hardre & Reeve, 2003).

3.6.4 General Causality Orientation Scale (GCOS)

General Causality Orientation Scale (GCOS): Causality orientations within SDT are conceptualized as enduring aspects of humans that characterize the source of imitation and regulation (see Appendix F). The GCOS (Deci & Ryan, 1985) was designed to assess three different motivational orientations, autonomy, control and impersonal. The scale has been shown to be reliable, with Cronbach's alpha of about 0. 75 and a test-retest coefficient of 0. 74 over two months.

It was consisted of twelve vignettes, each with three options to response, depending on an individual's orientation towards autonomy, control and impersonal. Respondents responded on total of 36 items on six-point Likert scale ranging from 1 = very unlikely, to 6 = very likely, for the option that is typical for them.

3.6.5 Learning Climate Questionnaire (LCQ)

Learning Climate Questionnaire (LCQ): Autonomy support within SDT was referred to a learning environment where teachers facilitated congruence by identifying and nurturing students' needs, interests and preferences (Reeve, 2006). The focus of the study was to analyze the classroom environment which can vary in degree of autonomy support. LCQ was a questionnaire designed for the purpose of accessing the degree to which target individuals such as students, employees, perceive people in authority such as teacher, manager, to be autonomy supportive. LCQ yielded a score on six point Likert scale which indicated the degree to which teachers are perceived to be autonomy supportive by students (see Appendix G).

For the present study, a short six-item version was used to assess the degree to which the students perceived their teachers to be autonomy supportive. A higher score on scale represented a higher level of autonomy support. The scale(LCQ) had been used successfully in learning settings (Black & Deci, 2000). The alpha coefficient of internal consistently of LCQ was reported virtually above 0. 90. In the present study, the scale was used prior to intervention (classroom without TAS) as a pretest and after intervention (classroom with TAS) as a posttest, in order to examine students' perception for their teacher to be autonomy supportive or not.

3. 7　Procedures

3. 7. 1　Recruitment

The researcher of this study wrote a letter to the intervention school district education administration to show intent to collect data in the school district. In this letter, it also explained rational details about this research (see Appendix H). After that, the researcher had a meeting with the research committee and introduced the research objectives, the data collection requirements and the benefits of taking part in this research.

After the research committee of the school district approved the data collection, the researcher sent an introduction e-mail (information of researcher, research purposes, participation criteria and the advantages of participation) and determined the interest of the school district junior middle school principals. The project investigator randomly chose one school which was interested in this project. The principal from the selected school gave the project investigator authority to choose teachers to participate in this research.

The researcher used the General Causality Orientation Scale (GCOS) to choose teachers. The headmaster of participating school offered an agreement which indicated their commitment to the needs of this research, and during their psychological well-being classes, the Strong Kids course was implemented as a pilot course in their Grade 8 general education classroom.

3. 7. 2　Consent Processes

School of Education and Modern Language Universiti Utara Malaysia (SEML UUM), the school district's educational authority and the intervention school principal in China all approved consent and assent letters in this research.

Teachers read and signed consents to participate in this research at the in-service training (see Appendix I).

The student's consent form was provided at pretest time, before the interventions began. The student consent described and outlined the study and asked students to sign up before participating in this research (see Appendix J).

The data collector read the consent form for all students. Meanwhile, the data collector informed the students that it was voluntary to take part in this program and they have the authority to quit at any time. If necessary, students could ask questions. Those students who did not want to join the program, were guided to another classroom to study independently during the course. In addition, those students did not take part in pretest and posttest.

The data collector gathered all consent letters during the pretest and take notes to make it easy for tracking. Students who did not take part in this research would be separately filed and were not included for data analysis. Teachers also did not allow those students to participate in Strong Kids activities or teacher autonomy supportive Strong Kids' activities.

3.7.3 Teacher Training

About two weeks before data collection, teachers received on-the-job training on this research project, with particular emphasis on the implementation of Strong Kids curriculum. There were two separate training sessions, one for teachers who implemented the original Strong Kids curriculum and the other for teachers who implemented Strong Kids in a teacher autonomy supportive way.

3.7.3.1 Original Strong Kids Teacher Training

For the initial Strong Kids intervention teacher training, the researcher of this study summarized the research on social and emotional learning, the theoretical basis of Strong Kids curriculum, the organization and materials required for each class, the components or techniques to be taught for each class, and presented the dependent measures used for pretest and posttest. Teachers participating in the training received in-depth training on the original 12 Strong Kids lessons, discussing the activities and supplements in each lesson. Project investigators reviewed and announced potential obstacles to implementation with teachers. Teachers were given the chance to ask further questions about related implementation issues. Teachers were told that the project investigators are available for implementation support throughout the project.

3.7.3.2   Teacher Autonomy Supportive Strong Kids Teacher Training

For the teacher autonomy supportive Strong Kids teacher training, except to know the content of the Strong Kids curriculum, they also learned a new technique. That is to teach Strong Kids in teacher autonomy support way. According to Cheon and Reeve(2018), there are three steps of Teacher Autonomy support Strong Kids Intervention Program.

Step one was an information demonstration. It introduced autonomous support teaching, compared autonomous support with teacher control, provided empirical evidence on the benefits of autonomous support and costs of control, and introduced the following recommended practice of autonomous support teaching method to teachers: at the beginning of each new lesson, teacher should give chance to allow students to share their personal experimental on a particular topic, such as students' failure experience in emotional control, and teachers should show acceptance to students' negative feelings. During the delivering of the teacher autonomy supportive Strong Kids intervention, teacher should give rations before asking students to complete particular activities, and should offer encouragement and praise to students in each class during the implementation.

Step two was technique learning of autonomy supportive instructions. The trainer described, modeled, explained, coached and scuffled " how to " implement every recommended teacher autonomy supportive teaching behavior. It also provided examples and techniques of how to transform control teaching behavior into autonomous support behavior, like changing controlling instruction from " Everyone must finish this task in 10 minutes, otherwise, you will be fanned" to "I suggest everyone try your best to finish this task in 10 minutes. I will be proud of you if you can do that!"

Step three was a group discussion to share the "how to" experience of each recommended teaching behavior. Teachers shared their classroom experience and exchange suggestions on how to become more autonomy supportive and reduce control over students in the teaching process.

During the training period, teachers were provided with all necessary research-based learning materials, which were organized with easy-to-carry cases, such as Strong Kids curriculum, teaching supplements and handouts. Supplementary, teaching materials, handouts and slides were copied for use by teachers during the teaching period. A total number of 222 copies of handouts used for lessons were produced for students. The student consent letter was reviewed during the training period. Teacher consent letter was reviewed and signed by participating teachers. Finally, teachers were provided with data collection and program implementation schedule (see Appendix K). All teachers started and completed the intervention with the same pace.

3.7.4　Four Groups Intervention

Experimental Group 1: Regular teacher with Strong Kids Intervention (RT + SEL).

Regular teacher in experimental group 1 delivered the original Strong Kids lesson, as following the instruction and procedure from the original Strong Kids curriculum. Time 1 data collection (pretest) occurred for experimental group 1 one week before the intervention (pretest). Time 2 data collection (posttest) occurred the following week of completing Lesson 12. As the students had psychological well-being class each week, the Strong Kids intervention was delivered in their psychological well-being class each week according to their class schedule. Each lesson took about 45 minutes to complete.

Experimental Group 2: Regular teacher with teacher autonomy supportive Strong Kids Intervention (RT + TASSEL).

Regular teacher in experimental group 2 delivered the teacher autonomy supportive Strong Kids intervention lesson, as following the instruction and procedure from the modified teacher autonomy supportive Strong Kids Intervention in this study. Time 1 data collection (pretest) occurred for experimental group 2 one week before the intervention (pretest). Time 2 data collection (posttest) occurred the following week of completing Lesson 12. As the students had psychological well-being class each week, the teacher autonomy supportive Strong Kids intervention was delivered in their psychological well-being class each week according to their class schedule. Each lesson took about 45 minutes to complete.

Experimental Group 3: Psychology teacher with Strong Kids Intervention (PT + SEL).

Psychology teacher in experimental group 3 delivered the original Strong Kids lesson, as following the instruction and procedure from the original Strong Kids curriculum. Time 1 data collection (pretest) occurred for experimental group 3 one week before the intervention (pretest). Time 2 data collection (posttest) occurred the following week of completing Lesson 12. As the students had psychological well-being class each week, the Strong Kids intervention was delivered in their psychological well-being class each week according to their class schedule. Each lesson took about 45 minutes to complete.

Experimental Group 4: Psychology teacher with teacher autonomy supportive Strong Kids Intervention (PT + TASSEL).

Psychology teacher in experimental group 4 delivered the teacher autonomy supportive Strong Kids intervention lesson, as following the instruction and procedure from the modified teacher autonomy supportive Strong Kids intervention in this study. Time 1 data collection (pretest) occurred for experimental group 4 one week before the intervention (pretest). Time 2 data collection (posttest) occurred the following week of completing Lesson 12. As the students had psychological well-being class each week, the teacher autonomy supportive Strong Kids intervention was delivered in their psychological well-being class each week according to their class schedule. Each lesson took about 45 minutes to complete.

3.7.5　Treatment Fidelity Check

3.7.5.1　Strong Kids Intervention Treatment Fidelity

Treatment fidelity, also known as treatment compliance, plays a vital role in research to ensure that treatment has been implemented as expected and that treatment has been accurately tested. Baer, Wolf and Risely (1987) argued that the importance of therapeutic fidelity lies in "recommending loyalty to the original process, which has been studied and is known to be effective. Their changes and substitutes are usually not studied, so there is nothing to say about their effectiveness (p. 321)".

In addition, treatment fidelity is critical to ensure internal effectiveness (reducing type I and II errors). By reducing the unexpected variability of treatment effect, the research power is improved by ensuring the fidelity of implementation. In addition, treatment loyalty supports external effectiveness because research can be replicated and disseminated.

Moreover, the benefits of ensuring treatment fidelity include linking assessment with intervention (Carta, 2002; Ingham & Riley, 1998); promoting cross-environmental promotion (Halle, 1998); ensuring and achieving lifestyle changes and social outcomes (Turnbull & Turnbull, 2000); enhancing the rigor of scientific research through building a functional relationship.

In this study, treatment fidelity was measured to ensure that the course was implemented as expected. Three Strong Kids courses (Lessons 1, 4 and 8) had corresponding treatment loyalty measures (see Appendix L). Teachers gave advance notice of each observation. The vice principal of the selected school who was in charge of teaching management conducted classroom-based observations directly to measure the fidelity of all participating teachers in the implementation of the established curriculum.

Observations lasted about 45 – 50 minutes throughout the course. The observer used the treatment checklist to approve the items on the checklist to indicate the degree of implementation of each component of each class. After each core component, the observer indicated whether the project under that component was "fully, partially or not implemented".

The fidelity of SEL implementation was determined by using the fully implemented items to divide the total number of all items into per class, and then multiply 100 percent to get fidelity percentage in each observation class, then add three observation class fidelity percentage together and divided three to get average fidelity percentage. Based on this method, SEL intervention fidelity in this study was 92 percent, which indicated the SEL intervention was implemented with high fidelity.

3.7.5.2   Teacher Autonomy Supportive Strong Kids Treatment Fidelity

In this study, in order to check the teacher autonomy-supportive behaviors, we used two methods to check. The first one was to use the teacher autonomy supportive treatment fidelity checklist to check (see Appendix M), the other method was to ask the students to fill the form of Learning Climate Questionnaire (LCQ; Williams & Deci, 1996), which was used to explore if teachers in TASSEL intervention group implemented SEL intervention in a teacher autonomy supportive way. According to our survey, we found teachers in TASSEL groups got higher score (mean = 3.15) than teacher in SEL intervention groups (mean = 2.62), and our observer also reported 93.5 percent TASSEL intervention fidelity, using the same method as SEL fidelity check to compute TASSEL fidelity percentage. Hence, we found in TASSEL intervention groups, teachers implemented teacher autonomy supportive behaviors, which fulfilled the requirement of teacher autonomy supportive fidelity check.

3.7.6   Pacing

Pacing. The rhythm of treatment was controlled by offering a week-by-week fidelity checklist, other than providing them with materials at the beginning of the program (see Appendix N). At the end of each course, each teacher received an email that included a weekly course reminder, an electronic copy of the fidelity checklist, and support to alleviate the burden on the course to move forward. The protocol was made once a week. The teachers delivered the classes according to the weekly email, and each lesson was expected to delivered 100 percent.

Throughout the project, project investigator maintained close contact with teachers under all conditions through e-mail and WeChat message and ensured timely support for teachers according to the allocation of treatment conditions by teachers. Project investigators sent a weekly schedule reminding teachers of their intervention. Project investigator also checked in with teachers by message or e-mail to obtain progress or answer any questions in the progress of the project.

Weekly message and e-mail registration by project investigator was important to pace the process of intervention. Check-in also held teachers accountable for their commitment to participation and allowed open communication in promoting successful implementation.

3.8 Data Collection

There were two times of data collection, pretest and posttest data collection. The pretest data collection was on 11th September 2019, which was completed one week before the intervention, and the posttest was finished on 26th Dec., 2019. All the data was collected online in the intervention school's computer lab. The data collector went to the computer lab one day before the data collection, and checked the computer one by one to make sure each computer was working well.

For all treatment groups, data collectors arrived at computer lab before starting the Strong Kids course. The data collector read the instructions aloud to all students for each questionnaire. Students were allowed to raise their hands for clarification or explanation. For students who asked questions had limited understanding of specific concepts, the data collector should tell them to do their best to respond, and there were no correct or wrong answers.

During the data collection procedure, students were not allowed to discuss about the answer of survey. They could just give their personal answer, and there was no right or wrong answer, and if students did not finish answering all of the questions, the students could not submit their survey. In this way, there was no missing value, which means that all students have finished all the questions.

3.9   Data Analysis

In the current study, factorial design was utilized to investigate the effects of teacher type and intervention type based on Strong Kids curriculum intervention on junior middle school students' SEL knowledge, learning anxiety and dropout intention in rural southwest of China. The independent variables for this study are four different kinds of interventions.

The three dependent variables are student's SEL knowledge, as measured by SEL knowledge Test; learning anxiety, as measured by learning anxiety; dropout intention, as measured by dropout intention.

The Statistical Package for the Social Sciences (SPSS) version 25.0 was used to run the data analysis. In this research, for the purpose of testing the robustness of measurements, Cronbach's alpha was calculated for every instrument to check reliability for internal consistency. There were also descriptive statistics which included means, standard deviations, Skewness and Kurtosis of the variables examined in the pilot study.

In the main study, Cronbach's alpha was calculated to check the reliability of the instruments. Exploratory factor analysis (EFA) was applied for instrument validity check for SEL knowledge and dropout intention, as these two instruments have not been used in Chinese culture.

In order to test hypothesis of the present study, Multivariate Analysis of Variance (MANOVA) was used as main analysis. In this research, we used MANOVA because there were two independent variables (teacher type and intervention type) and three dependent variables examined simultaneously. However, there was no covariate used. That was why we did not apply MANOVA

(Leech, N. L., Barrett, K. C., & Morgan, G. A., 2005).

A 2 × 2 factorial MANOVA with pretest was to confirm the homogeneity of the four groups before intervention. A 2 × 2 factorial MANOVA with posttest was applied to find the main effect of teacher type, intervention type and interaction effect of teacher type and intervention type on the combination of all the dependent variables (SEL knowledge, learning anxiety and dropout intention). Finally, repeated measure Time × Group MANOVA was applied to find if there is main effect of time (pretest and posttest), main effect of groups, and interaction effect of Time × Group on the combination of all the dependent variables (SEL knowledge, learning anxiety and dropout intention). We also used post hoc analysis to differentiate the effects of the intervention on each dependent variable.

3.10　Pilot Study

It is vital to assess instruments' reliability and validity prior to the full-scale study. Accordingly, before conducting the final study, a pilot study was conducted with a sample of junior middle school students resembling the target population of this study. The pilot study was a test about the survey questions. In the pilot study, the survey questions are distributed to those people who are readily available or who volunteer to measure the arrangement of the survey questions or the range of ideas and opinions of the participants (Fowler, 2009). In the current research, we carried out the pilot study to ensure the validity and reliability of the variables included in our study. The data of this pilot were analyzed using SPSS version 25.0.

3.10.1　Sample for Pilot Study

153 junior middle school students were randomly chosen from a junior middle school which has homogenous feature of the main study populations. The demographic features of the respondents in the pilot study were similar to those of

the target population that are planned to be surveyed in the main study. A total of 153 online survey data were collected for the pilot study among the junior middle school students in Qinzhou City. The respondents were 54 males (35. 3 percent) and 99 females (64. 7 percent) aged from 13 to 15, and 82. 4 percent of them were in Grade Eight, 7. 2 percent in Grade Seven and 10. 4 percent in Grade Nine.

3. 10. 2   Pilot Data Collection Procedure

The questionnaires in the present study were translated into Chinese language in order to facilitate the understanding of the respondents. Back-to-back translation method was used in the present study (Brislin, R. W. , 1970). First, a Chinese professional psychological researcher who got her Ph. D. of Psychology in England translated all the original English questionnaires into Chinese, and then a second Chinese professional psychological researcher who is good at English translated them back into English.

After that, a third professional psychological researcher in Malaysia compared the back translation of English version questionnaires with the original English questionnaires and then made some comments on some words which may have different meanings. The first translator translated them into Chinese again, and then second translator back translated into English, until the third translator confirmed the back translated version have the same meaning with original English version. The questionnaires were administered in one rural junior middle school which was similar to intervention school. One teacher was trained to guide students to complete the online survey in the school computer lab. The students were given approximately 40 minutes to fill up the survey.

3. 10. 3   Results of Pilot Study

The results concerning descriptive statistics and reliability for all the instruments involved in our pilot study were computed through SPSS version 25. 0.

The results of the descriptive statistics such as the number of items, range, means values, standard deviations, alphas' values, skewness, and kurtosis values were exhibited in Table 3.11. Cronbach's Alpha was employed to demonstrate the internal consistency reliability of each scale. The values of Cronbach's alpha denote a high degree of internal consistency of the items; and the values above. 70 denote an adequate reliability coefficient (Kline, 2011).

According to the outcome of the present pilot study, alpha values ranging from 70 to 80, which signifies an adequate degree of internal consistency. Skewness and kurtosis values used to test the normal distribution of data. Leech, Barrett, and Morgan (2013) suggested a simpler way to check normal data distribution; if the values for skewness and kurtosis are within the range of -1.00 to $+1.00$ is acceptable. From the reported results in table 4.1, the skewness values are ranging from the lowest value of -0.66 to the highest value of -0.06; whereas, the kurtosis values are ranging from the lowest value of -0.60 to the highest value of 0.12 for all constructs. Since all values are within -1.00 to $+1.00$, which signifies normal distribution of the pilot data.

Table 3.11

Descriptive statistics and reliability analysis of constructs in the pilot study

Variables	Items	Range	M	SD	Alpha	Skewness	Kurtosis
SEL knowledge	20	0 - 20	12.1	3.21	0.70	-0.65	0.12
Learning anxiety index	15	0 - 15	9.23	3.40	0.80	-0.66	0.03
Dropout intention	3	1 - 6	3.46	1.33	0.80	-0.06	-0.60

3.11　Summary

Chapter three described the research methods in this study. It began with research design, which was a 2×2 quasi-factorial design. There were two levels of interventions. One was original Strong Kids intervention, the other one was teacher autonomy supportive social and emotional learning intervention. There were two levels of teachers. One was psychology teacher and the other one was regular teacher.

The independent variables were four different interventions, SEL intervention delivered by regular teacher, SEL intervention delivered by psychology teacher, teacher autonomy supportive SEL intervention delivered by regular teacher, teacher autonomy supportive SEL intervention delivered by psychology teacher. There were three dependent variables and measures, including student's SEL knowledge, as measured by SEL knowledge Test; Learning Anxiety, as measured by Learning Anxiety; dropout intention, as measured by dropout intention.

As this was a quasi-experiment research, so validity threat control of internal validity threat and external validity threat control were important to guarantee the effectiveness of the intervention. There were ten internal validity threat controls and three external validity threat controls, and each of these validity threats was controlled by the proper solution in the experiment design.

There were two treatment fidelities to guarantee that the interventions were implemented as expected. The first treatment fidelity was Strong Kids intervention treatment fidelity; SEL lesson fidelity checklist was used to identify if the interventions were delivered by 100 percent. The second treatment fidelity was teacher autonomy support treatment fidelity. Perceived teacher autonomy support questionnaire and TASSEL lesson fidelity checklist were used to measure teacher autonomy support; to identify if teacher autonomy supportive instruction was 100 percent delivered by instructors. In addition, we also have pacing to further the fidelity check.

In this study, the intervention procedures included recruitment, instructor training, consent procedures, intervention, data collection and pacing. The data analysis method in this study was descriptive statistics, factorial MANOVA and repeated measure MANOVA.

CHAPTER FOUR
RESULTS

4. 1 Introduction

This chapter presented the outcomes of this research. The chapter presented the results of experimental intervention, including preliminary analysis such as profiles of respondents, data screening procedures, descriptive statistics, reliability exploratory factor analysis, MANOVA data analysis, learning anxiety percentage and dropout intention percentage from pretest to posttest, and summary of hypotheses.

4. 2 Main Study

4. 2. 1 Sample for Main Study

The main study was conducted in Qinzhou City in southwest of China. Qinzhou City is one of the poorest places in the country, with a high dropout rate in rural junior middle schools. Out of 200 junior middle schools in the city, one boarding school was randomly chosen as intervention school to implement the study. A total number of 209 students (107 boys, 102 girls) from Grade 8 were recruited to participate in the current research. The average age is 14. 3 years old.

Out of seven classes in Grade 8, four classes were randomly chosen to conduct the experiments.

4. 2. 2   Data Collection and Response Rate

The process of data collection began in early September, 2019 and ended in December 2019. The duration for this intervention lasted 4 months. During the pretest, there were 222 participants who responded the online survey in the computer lab in the intervention school, and there were 216 participants took part in the posttest online survey. 6 participants missed during the posttest. The retrieved surveys resulted in a very satisfactory response rate of 97. 30 percent.

4. 2. 3   Profiles of Respondents

As stated earlier in this chapter (see data collection and response rate section), the response rate was 97. 30 percent (216 participants). After data screening procedure, followed the suggested thresholds of z-score > 3. 29 and Mahalanobis distance $p < 0.001$ as the criterion to detect univariate and multivariate outliers respectively (Tabachnick & Fidell, 2013), a total of 7 (4 univariate and 3 multivariate) outliers were eliminated from the data set. This left the final data with a set of 209 respondents to further the main analyses and answered the research questions. A summary of the descriptive statistics for all demographic variables is provided in Table 4. 1.

Table 4. 1

Summary of participants' profiles

Variables	Category	Frequency	Percentage
Gender	Male	107	51. 2
	Female	102	48. 8
Age	13	32	15. 3
	14	85	40. 7

Continued table

Variables	Category	Frequency	Percentage
	15	71	34.0
	16	17	8.1
	17	4	1.9
Number of children	1	5	2.4
	2	35	16.7
	3	90	43.1
	>3	79	37.8
Monthly income	<3000 RM	160	76.6
	3001-5000 RM	36	17.2
	5001-6000 RM	7	3.3
	>6,001 RM	6	2.9
Father work in city more than 6 months	Yes	73	34.9
	No	136	65.1
Mother work in city more than 6 months	Yes	91	43.5
	No	118	56.5
Father education	Primary school	100	47.8
	Junior middle school	90	43.1
	High school	14	6.7
	Degree and above	5	2.4
Mother education	Primary school	112	53.6
	Junior middle school	82	39.2
	High school	11	5.3
	Degree and above	4	1.9
Total		209	100

$N = 209$

From Table 4.1, we can see that there were 51.2 percent ($n = 107$) of male participants and 48. 8 percent (n = 102) of female participants, which demonstrated that the number of boys and girls in the present study was similar. In terms of age (Mean = 14. 3 , SD = 0. 91) , the participants were divided into four groups of the age range. Most of the participants were from the age of 14 to 15 years old, which represented 40. 7 percent (n = 85) and 34. 0 percent (n = 71) respectively, followed by the age group of 13 which represented 15. 3 percent (n = 32) , and age group of 16 which represented 8. 1 percent (n = 17) and age group of 17 which represented 1. 9 percent (n = 4) .

The percentage of participants who were the only child in their family was 2. 4 percent (n = 5) , the percentage of participants who had two kids in their family was 16. 7 percent (n = 35) , the percentage of participants who had three kids in their family was 43. 1 percent (n = 90) , the percentage of participants who had more than three children in their family was 37. 8 percent (n = 79) .

The participants whose family monthly income was less than 3000 *yuan* per month was 76. 6 percent (n = 160) , the participants whose family monthly income was 3001 − 5000 *yuan* per month was 17. 2 percent (n = 36) , the participants whose family monthly income was 5001 − 6000 *yuan* per month was 3. 3 percent (n = 7) , the participants whose family monthly income was more than 6001 *yuan* per month was 2. 9 percent (n = 6) .

The participants whose father worked in the city more than 6 months was 34. 9 percent (n = 73) , the participants whose father did not work in city more than 6 months was 65. 1 percent (n = 136). The participants whose mother worked in city more than 6 months was 43. 5 percent (n = 91) , the participants whose mother did not work in city more than 6 months was 56. 5 percent (n = 118).

The participants whose father's education was primary school was 47. 8 percent (n = 100) , the participants whose father's education was junior middle school was 43. 1 percent (n = 90) , the participants whose father's education was high school was 6. 7 percent (n = 14) , the participants whose father's education was degree and above was 2. 4 percent (n = 5). The participants whose mother's education was primary school was 53. 6 percent (n = 112) , the participants whose mother's education was junior middle school was 39. 2 percent ($n = 82$), the participants whose mother's education was high school was 5. 3 percent ($n = 11$), the participants whose mother's education was degree and above was 1. 9 percent ($n = 4$).

From the demographic information of participants, we can see that the average age of participants was 14. 3 years old, and the majority of them from low income families with two or more siblings, and the majority of their parents' education level was lower than high school, and more than a third of their parents worked in the cities more than half an year. According to previous literature review, all of these characteristics were dangerous signals for rural junior middle school students to have mental health problems and have the idea to drop out of school (Wang, et al. 2015, 2016).

4. 2. 4   Data Screening Procedures

After the data collection, the first step was screening the obtained data to optimize the usage of data and consider all the issues that could influence the data analyses. Following Tabachnick and Fidell (2013) recommendations for data analysis, a series of data screening process were conducted in several steps: a check on the precision of data entry, observing missing values in the data; as well as, fulfilling the multivariate analysis' assumptions such as testing normality, detecting univariate and multivariate outliers.

4. 2. 4. 1   Accuracy of Data Input

All the data were completed by online survey, and participants had to answer each question before they submitted online survey, otherwise, the computer would not allow the students to submit. After the participants completed their online survey, the researcher downloaded the data, and so there was no need to manually input data, and confirmed the accuracy of data input. All statistical values were within the range and did not indicate any issues concerning the data entry procedure. Besides, there was no peculiar value or out-of-range values within the data for the other variables (demographic information) involved in the questionnaire.

4. 2. 4. 2   Analysis of Missing Values

Missing data is a widespread problematic issue in all types of survey research because it usually involves a large sample size. Missing values usually emerge when the data is lost, respondents skipped questions, or they refused to complete some sensitive items (Creswell, 2012). Many analytical techniques do not tolerate data with missing values and could be problematic (Leech et al. , 2013). Although there are no clear set guidelines regarding what constitutes a large number of missing values in the data; Kline (2011) suggested that the percentage of missing values less than 5 percent on a single construct in a large sample of participants is not problematic in the statistical analysis. In this research, the descriptive statistics analysis in terms of frequency analysis using SPSS software was applied to discover the missing values. The results demonstrated that there were no missing values in any of the variables, as the online survey required participants to answer each question before submission. Therefore, there was no missing value, all the data were treated as normal data.

4. 2. 5   Assumptions for Multivariate Analysis

The statistical procedure for performing MANOVA requires some serious considerations. Violation of these assumptions can mislead the outcome of the final analysis. The issues regarding MANOVA assumptions as identified by Tabachnick and Fidell's (2007) are: unequal sample size, multivariate normality, univariate outliers, multivariate outliers, multicollinearity and singularity and homogeneity of covariance.

4. 2. 5. 1   Unequal Sample Size

MANOVA requires sufficient number of sample sizes in each cell to ensure adequate power. It is necessary to have more cases than dependent variable in every cell or else for analysis homogeneity of covariance. Cells become singular and the assumption remains untestable. Also, a dissatisfactory cases-to-dependent variable ratio is capable of lowering the power of analysis because of reduced degree of freedom for error. In the present study, the groups are made from intact classroom; each class had more than 50 participants, therefore, this condition satisfied equal cases to dependent variable ratio in all sets of tests.

4.2.5.2 Multivariate Normality

Normal distribution of the data is an important early step because it is an assumption of many statistics, and it is imperative to be measured and addressed before performing inferential analyses.

Table 4.2

Values of skewness and kurtosis

Scale	No. of items	Range	Skewness	Kurtosis
SEL knowledge	20	0 – 20	− 0.24	− 0.73
Learning anxiety index	15	0 – 15	− 0.48	− 0.30
Dropout intention	3	1 – 6	− 0.09	− 0.27

$N = 209$

Table 4.2 presented the values of skewness and kurtosis, which considered as the two main components to check the normal distribution of the data. For skewness and kurtosis, if the z-value does not exceed the value of ± 2.58, the data is normally distributed. The z-score is calculated by way of dividing the statistics of skewness and kurtosis by their standard error. However, Leech et al. (2013) suggested a simpler way to check normality rather than using manual calculation; that is, the data is normally distributed if the values for skewness and kurtosis are within − 1.00 to + 1.00. According to the above table, skewness values are ranging from − 0.48 to − 0.09, and the kurtosis values are ranging from − 0.73 to − 0.27; thus, all measured variables in this research revealed a normal distribution of their data.

4. 2. 5. 3   Univariate Outliers

Univariate outliers are the cases with extreme values that deviate from other observations on one variable which can have a deleterious influence on the outcome of the statistical analyses. According to Tabachnick and Fidell (2013), any case with standardized scores of the measured variable exceeding ± 3.29 ($p < 0.001$) is considered as a potential outlier on that variable. In the present study, z score values of the substantive variables were calculated. The results showed that z score values for all variables were within the range from -3.29 to $+3.29$, except 4 cases were disconnected from other cases. By this criterion, 4 of the 216 cases were identified as univariate outliers; thus, those participants were deleted from our data set, leaving a total number of 212 as sample size.

4. 2. 5. 4   Multivariate Outliers

Multivariate outliers are cases with an unusual or such a strange combination of values over multiple variables that can undesirably distort the statistical results (Byrne, 2016). Thus, it is imperative to examine data for such elements and offer a remedy if they exist in our data set to perform ideal inferential statistics. A common approach to detect multivariate outliers is computing the squared Mahalanobis distance at $p < 0.001$ for each case in the data set (Byrne, 2010). Through regression command in SPSS, all cases with a Mahalanobis distance value that exceed the upper critical value of chi-square distribution with 8 degrees of freedom (following the number of variables), $\chi2$ (5, 0.001) $= 20.52$, are observed as multivariate outliers and should be omitted (Tabachnick & Fidell, 2013). Based on this criterion, out of 212 cases, 3 cases reported values higher than 20.52. These 3 cases were considered as multivariate outliers and were deleted; thus, leaving a final sample size of 209.

4. 2. 5. 5   Test of Multicollinearity and Singularity

Multicollinearity (or collinearity) occurs when there are high inter-correlations among various predictor variables which can lead to statistical instability or/and inaccurate statistical results. The threshold values that suggest serious multicollinearity are < 0.1 for tolerance and > 10 for the Variance Inflation Factor (VIF) (Kline, 2011). Furthermore, singularity and multicollinearity occur when there are high correlations among a set of independent variables (r = 0.90 and above) (Tabachnick & Fidell, 2013). As provided in SPSS version 25.0, the collinearity diagnostic was conducted. Table 4.3 demonstrated that the tolerance value is 0.99, and the highest VIF value is 1.02, which were in the recommended range.

Table 4.3

Tolerance and VIF of all dependent variables

Independent variable	Tolerance	VIF
SEL knowledge	0.99	1.01
Learning anxiety	0.99	1.01
Dropout intention	0.99	1.02

In addition, the correlations between all the predictors ranged between the lowest r = −0.13 to the highest r = 0.17 (p < 0.01), as shown in Table 4.4. There was no value exceeding r = 0.90. Therefore, there was no indication of the presence of multicollinearity and singularity among variables of the current study.

Table 4.4

Correlation matrix

Scale	SEL knowledge	Learning anxiety	Dropout intention
SEL knowledge	1.00		
Learning anxiety	0.05	1.00	
Dropout intention	0.17 *	−0.13 *	1.00

Note: N = 209; *. Correlation is significant at the 0.05 level (2-tailed).

We also conducted Mardia's test to check the multivariate normality, for SEL knowledge, learning anxiety and dropout intention. The Shapiro-Wilk was significant (P > 0.05), which meant that the variables at pretest are normally distributed.

4. 2. 5. 6   Homogeneity of Covariance

The test of homogeneity of covariance was conducted prior to the multivariate analysis of variance for testing the group differences. SPSS generates Box's M statistics at $p < 0.001$ to check if there is any significant difference. Details on Box's M statistics were given in the relevant sub sections that reported the results for the multivariate analysis of variance. Therefore, prior to running the main analysis, all assumptions check for MANOVA such as sample size, multivariate normality, univariate outliers, multivariate outliers, multicollinearity and singularity, and homogeneity of covariance were performed and were found to be satisfactory.

4. 2. 6   Reliability and Descriptive Analysis for Scales

To investigate the consistency of responses, the internal consistency of each variable in the instrument was tested by observing Cronbach's alpha values. Descriptive statistics, such as the number of items, range, Cronbach's alpha values, means, and Standards Deviation (SD) concerning each scale are shown in Table 4. 5. As exhibited in the table, all the measurement variables had high Cronbach's alpha values which ranged from 0. 76 to 0. 78.

Table 4. 5

Summary statistics for scales

Scale	No. of items	Range	Alpha	Mean	SD
SEL knowledge	20	0 – 20	0. 76	11. 57	3. 10
Learning anxiety index	15	0 – 15	0. 77	9. 63	3. 58
Dropout intention	3	1 – 6	0. 78	10. 46	3. 71

$N = 209$

In order to confirm the reliability and validity of instruments, it is necessary to complete psychometric assessment such as exploratory factor analysis with translated items in the instruments (Hambleton, et al. , 2004).

In this research, the learning anxiety instrument is the most widely used scale to measure the anxiety of junior middle school students in China (Yao et al., 2011; Zhou, 1991). The reliability of LA ranges from 0.84 to 0.88, and that of retest ranges from 0.78 to 0.86 (Yao et al., 2011). So, we adopted the Chinese version of learning anxiety questionnaire. However, both SEL knowledge and dropout intention questionnaires had not been used in Chinese culture. As a result, both SEL knowledge and dropout intention instruments were all translated into Chinese by back-to-back translation method, so it was necessary to complete psychometric assessment of exploratory factor analysis on these two instruments.

4.2.7 Exploratory Factor Analysis

Factor analysis is a data reduction technique used to reduce a large number of variables to a smaller set of underlying factors that summarize the essential information contained in the variables. More frequently, factor analysis is used as a technique when the researcher wishes to summarize the structure of a set of variables. When the researcher's goal is to construct a reliable test, factor analysis is an additional means of determining whether items are tapping into the same construct. One of the most frequently used methods of factor extraction is Principal Axis Factoring (PAF). In this research, a Principal Axis Factoring (PAF) extraction method and oblique rotation using varimax method were employed on the 20 items of SEL knowledge. See Table 4.6.

Table 4. 6

Exploratory factor analysis for SEL knowledge: factor loadings
based on Principal Axis Factoring and varimax rotation method

	Factors loadings						
Items	Factor 1 Positive living	Factor 2 Reduce stress	Factor 3 Clear thinking	Factor 4 Understand emotion	Factor 5 Smart goals	Factor 6 Anger handle	Factor 7 Problem solve
SKK20	0. 70						
SKK13	0. 64						
SKK 7	0. 57						
SKK18	0. 51						
SKK16		0. 74					
SKK9		0. 71					
SKK15		0. 56					
SKK8			0. 59				
SKK2			0. 58				
SKK11			0. 51				
SKK6				0. 66			
SKK4				0. 59			
SKK3				0. 52			
SKK10				0. 46			
SKK19					0. 76		
SKK12					0. 64		
SKK17						0. 81	
SKK14						0. 45	
SKK1							0. 75
SKK5							0. 45
Total Eigenvalues	2. 95	1. 56	1. 37	1. 28	1. 17	1. 08	1. 02

Continued   table

Factors loadings							
Percentage of variance explained	14. 76	7. 82	6. 84	6. 37	5. 87	5. 39	5. 10
KMO		0. 70					
Bartlett's test of sphericity		* 498. 85					
Df		190					
Total variance explained		52. 15					

$N = 209$

The factor extraction analysis of these items was forced to provide a seven-factor solution based on the definition of SEL knowledge (Feuerborn, 2004). The factor loadings of all items with absolute values of 0. 40 and above (Reio & Shuck, 2015) were accepted as adequate items to constitute a meaningful and interpretable factor and contribute significantly towards explaining each of the SEL knowledge constructs.

Table 4. 6 showed the seven-factor solution for SEL knowledge using the Principal Axis Factoring (PAF) method of extraction and varimax statistical techniques. Based on the table, all twenty items loaded strongly on their targeted factor with loadings ranging from the minimum value of 0. 45 to the maximum value of 0. 81; as well as exceeded the recommended cut off value of 0. 40. This analysis also showed that Kaiser-Mayer-Olkin (KMO) revealed a value of 0. 70 with a degree of freedom of 190, and Bartlett's test of sphericity with a value of 498. 85 was significant at $p < 0.05$, which provided evidence of sampling adequacy and correlation matrix was not an identity matrix. Besides, the percentage of the total variance of the factor explained by the subjected items was 52. 15 percent. Hence, the whole items of this scale were valid and retained for the final analysis.

In this research, a Principal Axis Factoring (PAF) extraction method and oblique rotation using varimax method were employed on the three items of dropout intention. The factor extraction analysis of these three items was forced to provide a three factors solution based on the definition of dropout intention (Varelland 1997). The factor loadings of all items with absolute values of 0.40 and above (Reio & Shuck, 2015) were accepted as adequate items to constitute a meaningful and interpretable factor and contribute significantly towards explaining each of the dropout intention construct.   See Table 4.7.

Table 4.7

Exploratory factor analysis for dropout intention; factor loadings
based on Principal Axis Factoring and varimax rotation method

Items	Factor 1 dropout intention
DOI 1	0.70
DOI 2	0.83
DOI 3	0.70
Total. Eigenvalues	2.09
Percentage of variance explained	69.50
KMO	0.69
Bartlett's test of sphericity	*180.55
df.	3
Total variance explained	69.50

$N = 209$

Table 4.7 showed the one-factor solution for dropout intention using the Principal Axis Factoring (PAF) method of extraction and varimax statistical techniques. Based on the table, all three items loaded strongly on their targeted factor with loadings ranging from the minimum value of 0.70 to the maximum value of 0.83; as well as exceeded the recommended cut off value of 0.40. This analysis also showed that Kaiser-Mayer-Olkin (KMO) revealed a value of 0.69 with a degree of freedom of 3, and Bartlett's test of sphericity with a value of 180.55 was significant at $p < 0.05$; which provided evidence of sampling adequacy and correlation matrix was not an identity matrix. Besides, the percentage of the total variance of the factor explained by the subjected items was 69. 50 percent. Hence, the whole items of this scale were valid and retained for the final analysis.

4.2.8 MANOVA

On the basis of research design with multiple variables, and more than one group analysis, the present study relied on MANOVA as main analysis in order to study group differences that should have occurred as a result of intervention. MANOVA in this condition was deemed appropriate to capture any significant differences that have occurred within and between groups as an interaction effect of multiple correlated dependent variables; it also helped in protecting against inflated Type I error (Tabachnick & Fidell, 2007). MANOVA is sensitive to various assumptions. These assumptions and their findings were found to be satisfactory.

4.2.8.1   MANOVA: Prior to Intervention

To assess whether regular teacher and psychology teacher with SEL and TASSEL have different scores at pretest on the combination of SEL knowledge, learning anxiety and dropout intention, a multivariate analysis of variance was conducted with pretest.

4.2.8.1.1   Descriptive Statistic of Four Groups for Pretest

The first order of analysis began with checking the assumption that all the four groups represented a homogeneous population. Following Table 4.8, a summary of means and standard deviations for SEL knowledge, learning anxiety and dropout intention at pretest.

Table 4. 8

Summary of means and standard deviations for SEL knowledge, learning anxiety and dropout intention at pretest as a function of teacher type and intervention type

Teacher type	Intervention type	n	SEL knowledge	Learning anxiety	Dropout intention
Regular teacher	SEL	51	11. 37 (3. 05)	9. 78 (3. 63)	10. 24 (3. 96)
Regular teacher	TASSEL	55	11. 29 (3. 30)	9. 36 (3. 79)	11. 36 (3. 72)
Psychology teacher	SEL	50	11. 84 (3. 07)	10. 06 (3. 82)	10. 06 (3. 91)
Psychology teacher	TASSEL	53	11. 79 (3. 02)	9. 34 (3. 09)	10. 11 (3. 17)

4. 2. 8. 1. 2   Between Group Differences at Pretest

A between group MANOVA was performed on the combination of three dependent variables, namely SEL knowledge, learning anxiety and dropout intention for these four groups on pretest in order to examine if there was any significant difference among the four groups. Assumptions prior to running a MANOVA analyses were met as suggested by Tabachnick and Fidell (2007). The sample size for all the four groups was almost similar. As explained in assumption for multivariate analysis, a standardized z-score was performed to detect univariate outliers and Mahalanobis distance was calculated to detect multivariate outliers. There was no evidence of outliers. Also, the results of multicollinearity and singularity were satisfactory as VIF and tolerance values were within acceptable ranges. Box's M statistics suggested equality of covariance across groups at alpha level $p > 0.001$.

Table 4. 9

Differences between groups at pretest

		Value	F	df	Error df	Sig.	Partial eta squared
Group	Wilks' Lambda	0. 953	1. 106	3. 000	205	0. 36	0. 02

As shown in Table 4. 9, Wilks' lambda statistics was generated using SPSS. The omnibus multivariate results presented no significant difference (Wilks' λ = 0. 95, F (3, 205) = 1. 11, $p > 0.05$, $\eta2 = 0.02$) among the four groups on all three variables at pretest level. Therefore, it was assumed that all the groups came from a homogeneous population.

4.2.8.1.3 2 × 2 Factorial MANOVA before Intervention

After the testing of homogenous groups, we ran 2 × 2 *factorial MANOVA* to see if there were main effects of teacher type, intervention type and interaction effect of teacher type and intervention type on the combination of the SEL knowledge, learning anxiety and dropout intention at pretest, as demonstrated in Table 4.10, Figure 4.1, 4.2 and 4.3.

Table 4.10

Effects of teacher type, intervention type, interaction effect of teacher type and intervention type on the combination of the SEL knowledge, learning anxiety and dropout intention at pretest

Items		Value	F	df	Error df	Sig	Partial eta squared
Teacher type	Wilks' lambda	0.97	1.82	3	203	0.15	0.03
Intervention type	Wilks' lambda	0.99	0.92	3	203	0.43	0.01
Teacher type X Intervention type	Wilks' lambda	0.99	0.53	3	203	0.67	0.01

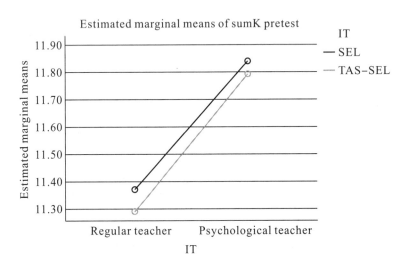

Figure 4.1   Interaction effect of teacher type and intervention type

on SEL knowledge at pretest

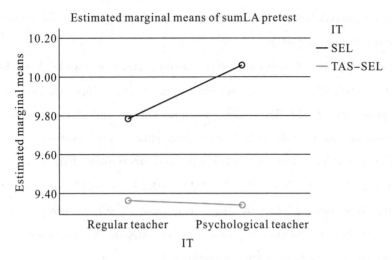

Figure 4. 2   Interaction effect of teacher type and intervention type

on learning anxiety at pretest

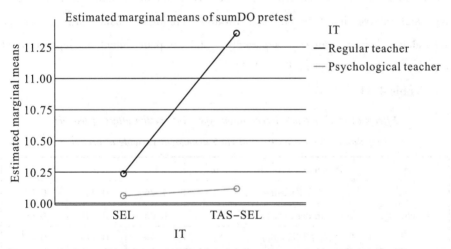

Figure 4. 3   Interaction effect of teacher type and intervention type

on dropout intention at pretest

The assumption of independence of observation and homogeneity of variance was checked and met. Bivariate scatterplots were checked for multivariate normality. From table 4. 11, we can see that the main effect of teacher type was not significant, Wilks' $\Lambda = 0.97$, F (3, 203) $= 1.82$, $p > 0.05$, multivariate $\eta2 = 0.03$. This indicated that the linear composite of SEL knowledge, learning anxiety and dropout intention at pretest did not differ between regular teacher and psychology teacher at pretest.

The main effect of intervention type was not significant, Wilks' $\Lambda = 0.98$, F (3, 203) $= 0.92$, $p > 0.05$, multivariate $\eta2 = 0.01$. This indicated that the linear composite of SEL knowledge, learning anxiety and dropout intention at pretest did not differ for different kinds of intervention type at pretest.

The interaction effect of teacher type and intervention type was also not significant, Wilks' $\Lambda = 0.99$, F (3, 203) $= 0.53$, $p > 0.05$, multivariate $\eta2$ $= 0.01$. This indicated that the linear composite of SEL knowledge, learning anxiety and dropout intention at pretest did not differ by the interaction effect of teacher type and intervention type at pretest.

Furthermore, we also ran follow-up MANOVA to see if there were significant main effects of intervention type, teacher type, and interaction effect of teacher type and intervention type on each variable separately, name SEL knowledge separately, learning anxiety separately, and dropout intention separately at pretest, as demonstrated in Table 4.11.

Table 4.11

Effects of teacher type, intervention type, interaction effect of teacher type and intervention type on each dependent variable at pretest

Source	Dependent variable	df	F	p	η
Teacher type	SEL knowledge	1	1.26	0.26	0.01
	Learning anxiety	1	0.06	0.80	0.00
	Dropout intention	1	1.94	0.17	0.01
Intervention type	SEL knowledge	1	0.02	0.88	0.00
	Learning anxiety	1	1.32	0.25	0.01
	Dropout intention	1	1.33	0.25	0.01
Teacher type × Intervention type	SEL knowledge	1	0.01	0.97	0.00
	Learning anxiety	1	0.09	0.76	0.00
	Dropout intention	1	1.10	0.30	0.01

Continued   table

Source	Dependent variable	df	F	p	η
	SEL knowledge	205			
Error	Learning anxiety	205			
	Dropout intention	205			

Table 4. 11 MANOVA test showed that for SEL knowledge, there was no significant main effect of teacher type, F (1, 205) = 1.26, $p > 0.05$, $\eta2 = 0.01$, no significant main effect of intervention type F (1, 205) = 0.02, $p > 0.05$, $\eta2 = 0.00$, and no significant interaction effect of teacher type and intervention type, F (1, 205) = 0.01, $p > 0.05$, $\eta2 = 0.00$.

For learning anxiety, there was no significant main effect of teacher type, F (1, 205) = 0.06, $p > 0.05$, $\eta2 = 0.00$, no significant main effect of intervention type, F (1, 205) = 1.32, $p > 0.05$, $\eta2 = 0.01$, and no significant interaction effect of teacher type and intervention type, F (1, 205) = 0.09, $p > 0.05$, $\eta2 = 0.00$.

For dropout intention, there was no significant main effect of teacher type, F (1, 205) = 1.94, $p > 0.05$, $\eta2 = 0.01$, no significant main effect of intervention type, F (1, 205) = 1.33, $p > 0.05$, $\eta2 = 0.01$, and no significant interaction effect of teacher type and intervention type, F (1, 205) = 1.10, $p > 0.05$, $\eta2 = 0.01$.

4.2.8.2   MANOVA: Post Intervention

To assess whether regular teacher and psychology teacher with SEL and TASSEL have different scores at posttest on the combination of SEL knowledge, learning anxiety and dropout intention, a 2 × 2 MANOVA was conducted at posttest level. The post intervention test was to answer research questions 1 to research question 3 in the present study.

RQ1 – Is there any significant main effect of teacher type (RT vs PT) on the combination of SEL Knowledge, learning anxiety and dropout intention at posttest?

RQ2 - Is there any significant main effect of intervention type (SEL vs TASSEL) on the combination of SEL Knowledge, learning anxiety and dropout intention at posttest?

RQ3 - Is there any significant interaction effect of teacher type (RT vs PT) and intervention type (SEL vs TASSEL) on the combination of SEL Knowledge, learning anxiety and dropout intention at posttest?

Parallel to research questions 1 - 3, the following hypotheses were postulated.

H1: There is significant main effect of teacher type (RT vs PT) on the combination of SEL Knowledge, learning anxiety and dropout intention at posttest.

H2: There is significant main effect of intervention type (SEL vs TASSEL) on the combination of SEL Knowledge, learning anxiety and dropout intention at posttest.

H3: There is significant interaction effect of teacher type (RT vs PT) and intervention type (SEL vs TASSEL) on the combination of SEL Knowledge, learning anxiety and dropout intention at posttest.

4.2.8.2.1　Descriptive Statistics for Four Groups at Posttest

Table 4.12 showed the summary of Means and Standard Deviations for SEL knowledge, learning anxiety and dropout intention at posttest.

Table 4.12

Summary of means and standard deviations for SEL knowledge, Learning anxiety and dropout intention at posttest as a function of teacher type and intervention type

Teacher type	Intervention type	n	SEL knowledge	Learning anxiety	Dropout intention
Regular teacher	SEL	51	12.16 (4.03)	9.63 (3.51)	9.71 (3.34)
Regular teacher	TASSEL	55	13.98 (3.42)	10.33 (3.23)	10.53 (2.94)
Psychology teacher	SEL	50	14.00 (3.39)	9.44 (3.00)	9.30 (3.79)
Psychology teacher	TASSEL	53	14.32 (3.73)	12.28 (2.47)	8.11 (2.72)

4.2.8.2.2　Group Differences at Posttest

SPSS was computed in order to find out the group difference at posttest by applying Wilks's lambda statistics. The omnibus multivariate results presented significant difference (Wilks' $\lambda = 0.78$, F $(3, 205) = 5.98$, $p < 0.001$, $\eta 2 = 0.08$) within the four groups on all three variables at posttest level, which meant there were significant differences among the four groups on the combination of all three constructs based on teacher type and intervention type. See Table 4.13.

Table 4.13

Differences between groups at posttest

		Value	F	df	Error df	Sig.	Partial eta squared
Group	Wilks' Lambda	0.78	5.98	3	205	0.000	0.080

4.2.8.2.3   2 × 2 Factorial MANOVA at Posttest

In order to examine the main effect of teacher type, intervention type and interaction effect of teacher type and intervention type on the combination of all variables, a 2 × 2 MANOVA was conducted at posttest, as demonstrated in Table 4.14, Figure 4.4, Figure 4.5 and Figure 4.6.

Table 4.14

Main effects of teacher type, intervention type, interaction effect of teacher type and intervention type on the combination of the SEL knowledge, learning anxiety and dropout intention at posttest

Items		Value	F	df	Error df	Sig	Partial eta squared
Teacher type	Wilks' Lambda	0.91	7.05	3	203	0.00	0.09
Intervention type	Wilks' Lambda	0.90	7.28	3	203	0.00	0.10
Teacher type × Intervention type	Wilks' Lambda	0.95	3.92	3	203	0.01	0.06

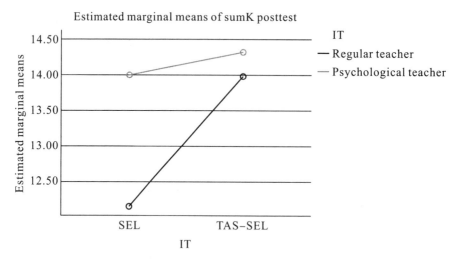

Figure 4. 4 Interaction effect of teacher type and intervention type on SEL knowledge at posttest

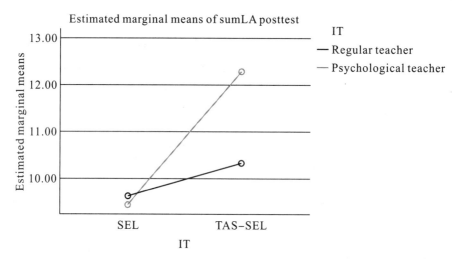

Figure 4. 5 Interaction effect of teacher type and intervention type on Learning anxiety at posttest

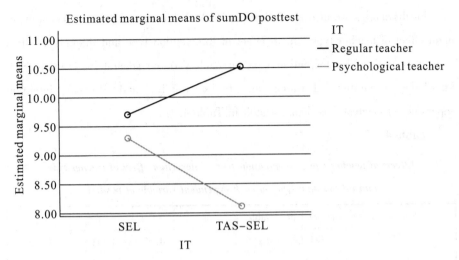

Figure 4. 6   Interaction effect of teacher type and intervention type on dropout intention at posttest

The assumption of independence of observation and homogeneity of variance was checked and met. Box's M statistics suggested equality of covariance across four groups at alpha level $p > 0.05$. Bivariate scatterplots were checked for multivariate normality.

From Table 4. 14, figure 4. 4, figure 4. 5 and figure 4. 6, we can see that the main effect of teacher type was significant, Wilks' $\Lambda = 0.91$, F $(3, 203)$ = 7. 05, $p < 0.001$, multivariate $\eta 2 = 0.09$. This indicated that the linear composite of SEL knowledge, learning anxiety and dropout intention at posttest differed for regular teacher and psychology teacher.

The main effect of intervention type was significant, Wilks' $\Lambda = 0.90$, F $(3, 203)$ = 7. 28, $p < 0.001$, multivariate $\eta 2 = 0.10$. This indicated that the linear composite of SEL knowledge, learning anxiety and dropout intention at posttest differed for different kind of intervention type.

The interaction effect of teacher type and intervention type was also significant, Wilks' $\Lambda = 0.95$, F $(3, 203)$ = 3. 92, $p < 0.05$, multivariate $\eta 2 = 0.06$. This indicated that the linear composite of SEL knowledge, learning anxiety and dropout intention at posttest differed by the interaction effect of teacher type.

Furthermore, we also ran follow-up MANOVA to see if there was significant main effect of teacher type, main effect of intervention type and interaction effect of teacher type and intervention type on each variable separately, namely SEL knowledge separately, learning anxiety separately, and dropout intention separately at posttest, as demonstrated in Table 4. 15.

Table 4. 15

Effects of teacher type, intervention type, interaction effect of teacher type and intervention type on each dependent variable at posttest

Source	Dependent variable	df	F	p	η
Teacher type	SEL knowledge	1	4. 67	0. 03 *	0. 02
	Learning anxiety	1	4. 31	0. 04 *	0. 02
	Dropout intention	1	10. 07	0. 00 **	0. 05
Intervention type	SEL knowledge	1	4. 51	0. 04 *	0. 02
	Learning anxiety	1	17. 31	0. 00 **	0. 08
	Dropout intention	1	0. 17	0. 68	0. 00
Teacher type X Intervention type	SEL knowledge	1	2. 22	0. 14	0. 01
	Learning anxiety	1	6. 34	0. 01 *	0. 03
	Dropout intention	1	5. 11	0. 03 *	0. 02
Error	SEL knowledge	205			
	Learning anxiety	205			
	Dropout intention	205			

$^*p < 0.05$, $^{**}p < 0.01$

From Table 4. 15, we can see that the Follow-up MANOVA test showed that for SEL knowledge, there was significant main effect of teacher type, F $(1, 205)$ $= 4. 67$, $p < 0. 05$, $\eta 2 = 0. 02$, significant main effect of intervention type F $(1, 205)$ $= 4. 51$, $p < 0. 05$, $\eta 2 = 0. 02$, no significant interaction effect of teacher type and intervention type on SEL knowledge, F $(1, 205)$ $= 2. 22$, $p > 0. 05$, $\eta 2 = 0. 01$.

We also checked simple interaction effect of teacher type and intervention type on SEL knowledge at posttest. See Table 4. 16.

Table 4. 16

Simple interaction effect of teacher type

and intervention type on SEL knowledge at posttest

TT * IT				IT * TT			
TT	IT	Mean	Std. Error	IT	TT	Mean	Std. Error
Regular teacher	SEL	12. 16	0. 51	SEL	Regular teacher	12. 16	0. 51
	TAS – SEL	13. 98	0. 52		Psychology teacher	14. 00	0. 52
Psychology Teacher	SEL	14. 00	0. 49	TAS – SEL	Regular teacher	13. 98	0. 49
	TAS – SEL	14. 32	0. 50		Psychology teacher	14. 32	0. 50

From pairwise comparisons, we found that for teacher type, when psychological teacher is concerned, there is no significant difference on the average score of SEL knowledge between SEL intervention and TASSEL intervention (14. 00 vs 14. 32). However, when regular teacher is concerned, there is significant difference on the average score of SEL knowledge between SEL intervention and TASSEL intervention (12. 16 vs 13. 98) (Mean Difference = $-1. 83^*$, $p < 0. 05$). TASSEL intervention has 1. 83 higher score than SEL on the condition of regular teacher.

From pairwise comparisons, we found that for intervention type, when TASSEL intervention is concerned, there is no significant difference on the average score of SEL knowledge between regular teacher and psychological teacher (13. 98 vs 14. 32). When the SEL intervention is concerned, there is significant difference on the average score of SEL knowledge between regular teacher and psychological teacher (12. 16 vs 14. 00) (Mean Difference = $-1. 84^*$, $p < 0. 05$). Psychological teacher has 1. 84 higher score than regular teacher on the condition of SEL intervention.

For learning anxiety, there was significant main effect of teacher type, $F (1, 205) = 4. 31$, $p < 0. 05$, $\eta2 = 0. 02$, significant main effect of intervention type, $F (1, 205) = 17. 31$, $p < 0. 01$, $\eta2 = 0. 08$, significant interaction effect of teacher type and intervention type F $(1, 205)$ $= 6.34$, $p < 0.05$, $\eta2 = 0.03$.

We also checked simple interaction effect of teacher type and intervention type on learning anxiety at posttest. See Table 4. 17.

Table 4. 17

Simple interaction effect of teacher type

and intervention type on learning anxiety at posttest

TT * IT				IT * TT			
TT	IT	Mean	Std. Error	IT	TT	Mean	Std. Error
Regular teacher	SEL	9. 63	0. 43	SEL	Regular teacher	9. 63	0. 43
	TAS – SEL	10. 33	0. 42		Psychology teacher	9. 44	0. 44
Psychology teacher	SEL	9. 44	0. 44	TAS – SEL	Regular teacher	10. 33	0. 42
	TAS – SEL	12. 28	0. 42		Psychology teacher	12. 28	0. 42

From pairwise comparisons, we found that for teacher type, when regular teacher is concerned, there is no significant difference on the average score of learning anxiety between SEL intervention and TASSEL intervention (9. 63 vs 10. 33). However, when psychological teacher is concerned, there is significant difference on the average score of learning anxiety between SEL intervention and TASSEL intervention (9. 44 vs 12. 28) (Mean Difference = − 2. 84 [*], $P <$ 0. 01). TASSEL intervention has 2. 84 higher score than SEL on the condition of psychological teacher.

From pairwise comparisons, we found that for intervention type, when SEL intervention is concerned, there is no significant difference on the average score of learning anxiety between regular teacher and psychological teacher (9. 63 vs 9. 44). However, when the TASSEL intervention is concerned, there is significant difference on the average score of learning anxiety between regular teacher and psychological teacher (10. 33 vs 12. 28) (Mean Difference = − 1. 96 [*], $p < 0.01$). Psychological teacher has 1. 96 higher score than regular teacher on the condition of TASSEL intervention.

For dropout intention, there was significant main effect of teacher type, F

$(1, 205) = 10.07$, $p < 0.01$, $\eta2 = 0.05$, no significant main effect of intervention type, F $(1, 205) = 0.17$, $p > 0.05$, $\eta2 = 0.00$, significant interaction effect of teacher type and intervention type, F $(1, 205) = 5.11$, $p < 0.05$, $\eta2 = 0.02$.

We also checked simple interaction effect of teacher type and intervention type on dropout intention at posttest. See Table 4. 18.

Table 4. 18

Simple interaction effect of teacher type and intervention type on dropout intention at posttest

TT * IT				IT * TT			
TT	IT	Mean	Std. Error	IT	TT	Mean	Std. Error
Regular teacher	SEL	9.71	0.45	SEL	Regular teacher	9.71	0.45
	TAS – SEL	10.53	0.43		Psychology teacher	9.30	0.45
Psychology teacher	SEL	9.30	0.45	TAS – SEL	Regular teacher	10.53	0.43
	TAS – SEL	8.11	0.44		Psychology teacher	8.11	0.44

From pairwise comparisons, we found that for teacher type, when regular teacher is concerned, there is no significant difference on the average score of dropout intention between SEL intervention and TASSEL intervention (9.71 vs 10.53). When psychological teacher is concerned, there is also no statistically significant difference on the average score of dropout intention between SEL intervention and TASSEL intervention (9.30 vs 8.11) (Mean Difference = −1.19, $P = 0.06$). Even though, TASSEL intervention has 1.19 higher score than SEL on the condition of psychological teacher.

From pairwise comparisons, we found that for intervention type, when SEL intervention is concerned, there is no significant difference on the average score of dropout intention between regular teacher and psychological teacher (9.71 vs 9.30). However, when the TASSEL intervention is concerned, there is significant difference on the average score of dropout intention between regular teacher and psychological teacher (10.53 vs 8.11) (Mean Difference = 2.41 *, $p < 0.01$). Psychological teacher has 2.41 lower score than regular teacher on the condition of TASSEL intervention.

4.2.8.3 Time × Group Repeated Measure MANOVA

A repeated measure MANOVA was conducted to assess if there was a significant main effect of time on the combination of SEL knowledge, learning anxiety and dropout intention from pretest to posttest in each group, if there were significant main effects of groups on the combination of SEL knowledge, learning anxiety and dropout intention among four groups from pretest to posttest and if there was significant intervention effect of Time × Group from pretest to posttest on the combination of dependent variables. The sample sizes were almost equal across the four groups, hence, the assumptions were considered to be met.

The repeated measure MANOVA test was applied to answer research questions 4 to research question 6.

RQ4 - Is there any significant main effect of groups on the combination of SEL knowledge, learning anxiety and dropout intention among four groups from pretest to posttest?

RQ5 - Is there any significant main effect of time on the combination of SEL knowledge, learning anxiety and dropout intention from pretest to posttest in each group?

RQ6 - Is there any significant interaction effect of Time × Group on the combination of SEL knowledge, learning anxiety and dropout intention from pretest to posttest?

Parallel to research questions 4 - 6, the following hypotheses were postulated.

H4: There is a significant main effect of groups on the combination of SEL knowledge, learning anxiety and dropout intention among four groups from pretest to posttest.

H5: There is a significant main effect of time on the combination of SEL knowledge, learning anxiety and dropout intention from pretest to posttest in each group.

H6: There is a significant intervention effect of Time × Group on the combination of SEL knowledge, learning anxiety and dropout intention from pretest to posttest.

4. 2. 8. 3. 1   Descriptive Statistics for Four Groups from Pretest to Posttest

Table 4. 19 showed the summary of comparisons of Means and Standard Deviations and gain score for SEL knowledge from pretest to posttest in four groups. Table 4. 20 and Table 4. 21 showed the summaries of comparisons of Means and Standard Deviations and reduction in scores for learning anxiety and dropout intention from pretest to posttest in four groups. It was analysis of gain or reduction in mean scores (mean difference from pretest to posttest) of all variables in four groups. The analysis of gain or reduction in mean scores provided unbiased results of true change in a much wider array of research design.

Table 4. 19

Summary of comparisons of means and standard deviations and gain score

for SEL knowledge from pretest to posttest in four groups

Group		n	SEL knowledge		
Teacher type	Intervention type	n	Pretest (1)	Posttest (2)	Difference (2) − (1)
Regular teacher	SEL	51	11. 37 (3. 05)	12. 16 (4. 03)	0. 79
Regular teacher	TASSEL	55	11. 29 (3. 30)	13. 98 (3. 42)	2. 69
Psychology teacher	SEL	50	11. 84 (3. 07)	14. 00 (3. 39)	2. 16
Psychology teacher	TASSEL	53	11. 79 (3. 02)	14. 32 (3. 73)	2. 53

Table 4. 20

Summary of comparisons of means and standard deviations and reduction in scores
for learning anxiety from pretest to posttest in four groups

Group		n	Learning anxiety		
Teacher type	Intervention type	n	Pretest (1)	Posttest (2)	Difference (2) - (1)
Regular teacher	SEL	51	9. 78 (3. 63)	9. 63 (3. 51)	-0. 15
Regular teacher	TASSEL	55	9. 36 (3. 79)	10. 33 (3. 23)	0. 97
Psychology teacher	SEL	50	10. 06 (3. 82)	9. 44 (3. 00)	-0. 62
Psychology teacher	TASSEL	53	9. 34 (3. 09)	12. 28 (2. 47)	2. 94

Table 4. 21

Summary of comparisons of means and standard deviations and reduction in scores
for dropout intention from pretest to posttest in four groups

Group		n	Dropout intention		
Teacher type	Intervention type	n	Pretest (1)	Posttest (2)	Difference (2) - (1)
Regular teacher	SEL	51	10. 24 (3. 96)	9. 71 (3. 34)	-0. 53
Regular teacher	TASSEL	55	11. 36 (3. 72)	10. 53 (2. 94)	-0. 83
Psychology teacher	SEL	50	10. 06 (3. 91)	9. 30 (3. 79)	-0. 76
Psychology teacher	TASSEL	53	10. 11 (3. 17)	8. 11 (2. 72)	-2. 00

4. 2. 8. 3. 2　Time × Group Repeated Measure MANOVA from pretest to posttest

After testing the homogenous of groups, we used Time × Group repeated measure MANOVA data analysis method to check if there was main effect of time, main effect of group and interaction effect of Time × Group on the combination of SEL knowledge, learning anxiety and dropout intention from pretest to posttest score, as demonstrated in Table 4. 22, Figure 4. 7, Figure 4. 8 and Figure 4. 9.

Table 4. 22

Time X group repeated measure MANOVA from pretest to posttest

		Value	F	Df	Error df	Sig.	Partial eta squared
Time	Wilks' Lambda	0. 74	23. 25	3	203. 00	0. 00	0. 26
Group	Wilks' Lambda	0. 86	3. 66	9	494. 20	0. 00	0. 05
Time X Group	Wilks' Lambda	0. 87	3. 11	9	494. 20	0. 00	0. 04

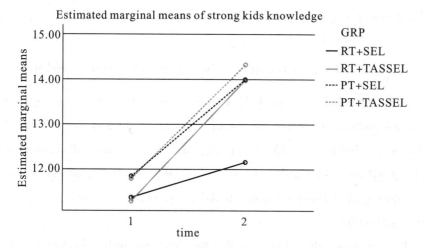

Figure 4. 7   Interaction effect of Time × group on SEL knowledge

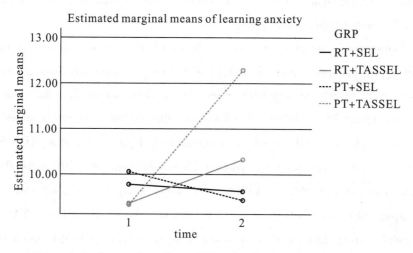

Figure 4. 8   Interaction effect of Time × Group on learning anxiety

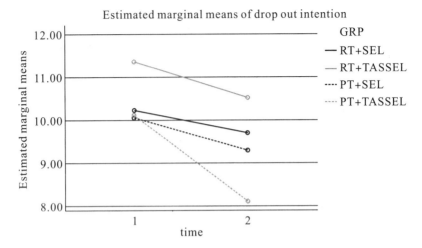

Figure 4.9 Interaction effect of Time × group on dropout intention

From Table 4.22, Figure 4.7, Figure 4.8 and Figure 4.9, we can see that significant multivariate effects were found for the main effect of time, Wilks' Λ = 0.74, F (3,205) = 23.25, $p < 0.01$, $\eta2 = 0.26$, main effect of groups, Wilks' Λ =0.86, F (3,205) =3.67, $p < 0.01$, $\eta2 = 0.05$, as well as for the interaction effect of Time × Group, Wilks' Λ =0.87, F (3,205) =3.11, $p < 0.01$, $\eta2 = 0.04$.

The interaction effect indicated that the difference within the four groups on the linear combination of the three dependent variables was different at posttest only, but was not different at pretest.

Furthermore, we also ran post hoc to check if there was significant main effect of time and interaction effect of Time × Group on each variable separately, namely SEL knowledge separately, learning anxiety separately, and dropout intention separately at posttest. Post hoc test indicated that, for SEL knowledge, PT + TASSEL intervention group had significantly higher score than RT + SEL intervention group from pretest to posttest (mean difference = 1.29, $p < 0.05$), which indicated that PT + TASSEL intervention group was a good choice at increasing SEL knowledge score. For dropout intention, PT + TASSEL intervention group had significantly lower score than RT + TASSEL group from pretest to posttest (mean difference = - 1.83, $p < 0.01$), which also implied that PT + TASSEL intervention group was a good choice to reduce dropout intention. However, for learning anxiety, there was no significant difference in four groups.

In a word, the Time × Group repeated measure test indicated that PT + TASSEL intervention group was the best choice to improve SEL knowledge and reduce dropout intention.

4.3 The Percentage of Learning Anxiety and Dropout Intention from Pretest to Posttest

From our research background and problem statement, the current study was on the aim to find a better way to reduce learning anxiety percentage and dropout intention percentage for Chinese rural junior middle schools, so we further calculated the percentage of the learning anxiety and dropout intention rate from pretest to posttest and compared the percentage to see if the present intervention can reduce learrning anxiety and dropout intention rate in each group, and which group has the best intervention effect to reduce learning anxiety percentage and dropout intention percentage from pretest to posttest.

For learning anxiety, a score more than 8 meant students have learning anxiety (Yao et al., 2011). Table 4.23 showed the percentage of participants' learning anxiety from pretest to posttest in four groups. For dropout intention, a score more than 3 meant that students have dropout intention (Hardre & Reeve, 2003). Table 4.24 demonstrated the percentage of participants' dropout intention from pretest to posttest in four groups. The percentage test was to answer research questions 7 to research question 8.

RQ7 - Is the present intervention effective in reducing rural junior middle school students' learning anxiety percentage from pretest to posttest?

RQ8 - Is the present intervention effective in reducing rural junior middle school students' dropout intention percentage from pretest to posttest?

Parallel to research questions 7 - 8, the following hypotheses were postulated.

H7: The present intervention is effective to reduce rural junior middle school students' learning anxiety percentage from pretest to posttest.

H8: The present intervention is effective to reduce rural junior middle school students' dropout intention percentage from pretest to posttest.

Table 4. 23

Percentage of participants' learning anxiety from pretest to posttest in four groups

Groups	n	Test	Pretest（1）	Posttest（2）	Difference (2) - (1)
Group 1 (RT + SEL)	51	Learning anxiety（LA）	62. 70 percent	58. 80 percent	-3. 90 percent
Group 2 (RT + TASSEL)	55	Learning anxiety（LA）	67. 30 percent	74. 50 percent	7. 20 percent
Group 3 (PT + SEL)	50	Learning anxiety（LA）	74 percent	66 percent	-8 percent
Group 4 (PT + TASSEL)	53	Learning anxiety（LA）	58. 50 percent	90. 60 percent	32. 10 percent

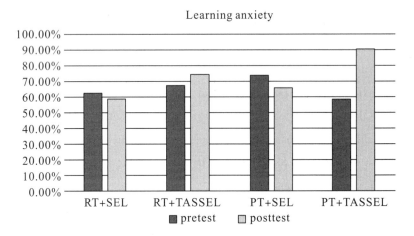

Figure 4. 10   Learning anxiety percentage in four groups from pretest to posttest

For the learning anxiety rate, our result was similar with previous studies, which have found junior high learning anxiety rate as high as 66 percent in rural China (Wang et al. , 2015).

From Table 4. 23 and Figure 4. 10, we can see that RT + SEL intervention group reduced learning anxiety by 3. 90 percent, RT + TASSEL intervention group increased learning anxiety by 7. 20 percent, PT + SEL intervention group reduced learning anxiety by 8 percent, PT + TASSEL intervention group increased learning anxiety by 32. 10 percent. Among the four groups, we can see that RT + SEL group and PT + SEL group had the ability to reduce rural junior middle school students' learning anxiety percentage, and these two groups reduced more than 2. 3 percent of learning anxiety, which was reported by Wang (2016) intervention effect. However, RT + TASSEL group and PT + TASSEL group could not reduce learning anxiety. Conversely, these two groups increased learning anxiety, as teacher autonomy support added psychological burden on Chinese students in class.

Table 4. 24

Percentage of participants' dropout intention from pretest to posttest in four groups

Groups	N	Test	Pretest (1)	Posttest (2)	Difference (2) − (1)
Group 1 (RT + SEL)	51	Dropout intention (DOI)	66. 70 percent	58. 80 percent	7. 90 percent
Group 2 (RT + TASSEL)	55	Dropout intention (DOI)	70. 90 percent	56. 40 percent	14. 50 percent
Group 3 (PT + SEL)	50	Dropout intention (DOI)	67. 00 percent	48. 30 percent	18. 70 percent
Group 4 (PT + TASSEL)	53	Dropout intention (DOI)	67. 90 percent	28. 30 percent	39. 60 percent

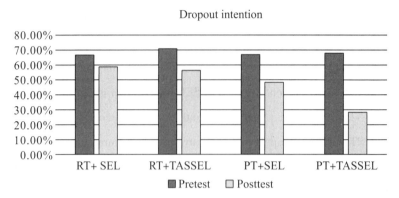

Figure 4. 11　Dropout intention percentage in four groups from pretest to posttest

For the dropout rate, our result was consistent with previous studies, which had found junior middle school dropout rates as high as 56 percent in rural China (Connelly & Zheng, 2003; Brown & Park, 2002).

From Table 4. 24 and Figure 11, we can see that RT + SEL intervention group reduced dropout intention by 7. 90 percent, RT + TASSEL intervention group reduced dropout intention by 14. 50 percent, PT + SEL intervention group reduced dropout intention by 18. 70 percent, PT + TASSEL intervention group reduced dropout intention by 39. 60 percent. Among the four groups, except RT + SEL intervention group, all other three groups had the ability to reduce rural junior middle school students' dropout intention percentage, and all the four groups reduced more than 1. 6 percent dropout intention, which was reported by Wang (2016) intervention effect. PT + TASSEL intervention group has reduced highest dropout intention percentage in the current study.

4. 4　Summary of Hypotheses

Table 4. 25

Summary of the acceptance or rejection of hypotheses

No.	Hypotheses statement	Decision
H1	There is significant main effect of teacher type（RT vs PT）on the combination of SEL Knowledge, learning anxiety and dropout intention at posttest.	Supported
H2	There is significant main effect of intervention type（SEL vs TASSEL）on the combination of SEL Knowledge, learning anxiety and dropout intention at posttest.	Supported
H3	There is significant interaction effect of teacher type（RT vs PT）and intervention type（SEL vs TASSEL）on the combination of SEL Knowledge, learning anxiety and dropout intention at posttest.	Supported
H4	There is significant main effect of groups on the combination of SEL knowledge, learning anxiety and dropout intention among four groups from pretest to posttest.	Supported
H5	There is significant main effect of time on the combination of SEL knowledge, learning anxiety and dropout intention from pretest to posttest in each group.	Supported
H6	There is significant interaction effect of Time × Group on the combination of SEL knowledge, learning anxiety and dropout intention from pretest to posttest.	Supported
H7	The present intervention is effective to reduce rural junior middle school students' learning anxiety percentage from pretest to posttest.	Supported
H8	The present intervention is effective to reduce rural junior middle school students' dropout intention percentage from pretest to posttest.	Supported

4. 5　Summary of Present Chapter

In this chapter, we highlighted the procedure of data analysis and presented the outcomes of this research to answer every research question. The overall purpose of the current study was to examine the effect of TASSEL intervention implemented by different teacher on junior middle school students' psychological health.

In chapter four, we demonstrated the obtained data and data analysis result based on the main study. We reported the population and sampling method of the main study and illustrated data collection procedure and response rate, followed with profile of respondents. Next, we reported data screening procedure which included accuracy of data input and analysis of missing value. After that we reported the assumption of MANOVA test, included sample size, multivariate normality, univariate outliers and multivariate outliers and test of multicollinearity and singularity and homogeneity of covariance. We also tested the reliability and descriptive analysis of scales and exploratory factor analysis (EFA) of scales which we translated to Chinese version by back-to-back translation, including SEL knowledge and dropout intention questionnaires.

As we had two factors, namely, teacher type and intervention type, and each factor had two levels, for teacher type we had regular teacher and psychology teacher; for intervention type, we had TASSEL and SEL, so we had a 2 × 2 factorial design which produced four groups, and also we had three dependent variables, namely SEL knowledge, learning anxiety and dropout intention. Each variable had pretest and posttest. In this case, we used three MANOVA data analysis method to analyze the data. The first one was 2 × 2 factorial MANOVA with pretest to identify if the four groups were homogeneous. The second one was 2 × 2 factorial MANOVA with posttest to identify if there was main effect of teacher type, main effect of intervention type and interaction effect of teacher type and intervention type on the combination of SEL knowledge, learning anxiety and dropout intention. The third one was Time X Group repeated measure MANOVA to identify if there was main effect of time, main effect of groups and interaction effect of Time X Group on the combination of SEL knowledge, learning anxiety and dropout intention.

Then we reported the three MANOVA result. Firstly, for the 2 × 2 factorial

MANOVA with pretest, we confirmed the homogeneous of all four groups, as the results showed that there was no main effect of teacher type, no main effect of intervention type, no interaction effect of teacher type and intervention type on the combination of SEL knowledge, learning anxiety and dropout intention at pretest.

Secondly, for the 2 × 2 factorial MANOVA with posttest, we found there was significant main effect of teacher type, significant main effect of intervention type, significant interaction effect of teacher type and intervention type on the combination of SEL knowledge, learning anxiety and dropout intention at posttest. Then, we used simple effect analysis to further explore the interaction of teacher type and intervention type to find the best group on increasing SEL knowledge, reducing learning anxiety and dropout intention. For SEL knowledge, the best interaction effect group is psychology teacher with teacher autonomy supportive SEL intervention group (PT + TASSEL). For learning anxiety, the best interaction group is psychology teacher with SEL intervention group (PT + SEL). For dropout intention, the best interaction effect group is psychology teacher with teacher autonomy supportive SEL intervention group (PT + TASSEL).

Thirdly, for Time X Group repeated measure MANOVA, the result showed there was significant main effect of time, significant main effect of groups, and significant interaction effect of Time X Group on the combination of SEL knowledge, learning anxiety and dropout intention, which meant that the interaction effect from pretest to posttest had significant difference within and between groups, and the post hoc test between groups showed that for both SEL knowledge and dropout intention, PT + TASSEL intervention group had the best intervention effect.

From the research background and problem statement, the current study was on the duty to find a better way to reduce learning anxiety and dropout rate for Chinese rural junior middle schools, so we further calculated the percentage of the learning anxiety and dropout intention rate from pretest to posttest and compared the percentage to see if the intervention can reduce leaning anxiety and dropout intention rate in each group, and which group had the best intervention effect to reduce learning anxiety and dropout intention.

Among the four groups, we found that RT + SEL group and PT + SEL group had the ability to reduce rural junior middle school students' learning anxiety percentage, and these two groups reduced more than 2. 3 percent of learning anxiety, which was reported by Wang (2016) intervention effect. The best group was PT + SEL group to reduce learning anxiety.

Among the four groups, except RT + SEL intervention group, all other three groups had the ability to reduce rural junior middle school students' dropout intention percentage, and all the four groups reduced more than 1. 6 percent dropout intention, which was reported by Wang (2016) intervention effect. PT + TASSEL intervention group was the best group to reduce dropout intention.

Finally, we gave a conclusion on the research hypothesis to check if we accepted or rejected our hypotheses in the current research. From the data analysis in this chapter, we can conclude that PT + TASSEL intervention group was the best choice to increase rural junior middle school students' SEL knowledge and reduce dropout intention and learning anxiety. PT + SEL intervention group is the best choice to reduce learning anxiety.

CHAPTER FIVE　DISCUSSION, IMPLICATION, LIMITATION AND RECOMMENTATION

5. 1　Introduction

This chapter described the discussions arising from the implementation of a Strong Kids based SEL curriculum with four different intervention groups within learners in rural junior middle school serving students in Grade 8. The chapter included the following sections: introduction, discussion, implication, limitations, future research recommendation and conclusion.

5. 2　Discussion

The chapter went further to discuss the main findings of the current studies. There were eight research questions in the present research. We discussed and explained the results for each question in detail.

5. 2. 1　Research Question 1: Is there significant main effect of teacher type (RT vs PT) on the combination of SEL knowledge, learning anxiety and dropout intention at posttest?

From Table 4. 14, the 2 × 2 MANOVA with posttest showed that there was a significant main effect of teacher type on the combination of SEL knowledge, learning anxiety and dropout intention at posttest.

We also conducted Follow-up MANOVA to identify the main effect of teacher type on each variable separately. For SEL knowledge, from Table 4.15, the Follow-up MANOVA test showed that there was a significant main effect of teacher type, F (1, 205) = 4.67, $p < 0.05$, η2 = 0.02. From Table 4.17, we can see that, for SEL knowledge, psychology teachers' average score was higher than regular teachers' average score, which meant that psychology teacher had better intervention effect on improving SEL knowledge. This result was reasonable, as psychology teachers are majored in psychology, they have more knowledge and skills about psychology, and can be better teacher to teach psychological knowledge like SEL knowledge.

The same result has been proven by several previous studies. Knof (1995) found that school psychology teachers are well-trained experts in psychological health and education in schools. Li (2017) revealed that school psychology teachers are more professional in implementing psychological intervention compared to regular school teachers. Ross et al. (2002) declared that school psychology teachers have a unique set of knowledge, techniques and abilities in assessing students' needs, designing and implementing intervention plans, and project evaluation.

When social and emotional learning intervention is concerned, it needs the school psychology teachers to have a set of specific knowledge and techniques, which are not necessarily shared by traditional classroom teachers. School psychology teachers must have a comprehensive understanding of the development of adolescents in order to influence behavior and knowledge of learning styles and behavior change. For example, SEL psychology teachers must know how to promote discussion on sensitive topics, such as anger management, how to build healthy relationships, how to reduce negative emotions, and reduce risk behaviors. In a word, school psychology teacher is more knowledgeable and skillful than regular teacher at improving Strong Kids intervention score.

For learning anxiety, from Table 4.15, the Follow-up MANOVA test showed that there was significant main effect of teacher type, $F_{(1, 205)}$ =4.31, $p <$ 0.05, $\eta2$ = 0.02. Table 4.17 showed that for learning anxiety, psychology teachers' average score was higher than regular teachers' average score. As regular teachers are main subjects teachers, and usually Chinese students consider main subjects teachers more important, as they can help with their examinations, which will help them reduce learning anxiety. However, psychology well-being class will not be included in their exams, so they do not feel psychology teacher can help them reduce learning anxiety, as Chinese students have great press under the high school entrance examination (HSEE) (Yi et al., 2012).

For dropout intention, from Table 4.15, the Follow-up MANOVA test showed there was significant main effect of teacher type, $F_{(1, 205)}$ =10.07, p < 0.01, $\eta2$ = 0.05. From Table 4.18, we can induce that, for dropout intention, psychology teachers' average score was lower than regular teachers', which meant psychology teachers had better intervention effect on reducing dropout intention.

This result was reasonable, as psychology teachers are majored in psychology, they have more psychological knowledge and technique to solve students' problem behaviors and thoughts, like dropout intention, especially when they used Strong Kids based intervention, as Strong Kids intervention was based on cognitive behavior theory (Merrell et al., 2008), which meant that if psychology teachers can improve students' psychological knowledge, they can change their thought and accordingly change their intention of behavior, like dropout intention.

In a word, from the above results, we can conclude that there was a significant main effect of teacher type on the combination of SEL knowledge, learning anxiety and dropout intention at posttest. Based on our further analysis on each dependent variable, we identified that except learning anxiety, psychology teachers were better than regular teachers at improving SEL knowledge and reducing dropout intention.

5.2.2 Research Question 2: Is there significant main effect of intervention type (SEL vs TASSEL) on the combination of SEL knowledge, learning anxiety and dropout intention at posttest?

From Table 4.14, the 2 × 2 MANOVA with posttest showed that there was a significant main effect of intervention type on the combination of SEL knowledge, learning anxiety and dropout intention at posttest, Wilks' $\Lambda = 0.90$, F $(3, 203)$ $= 7.28$, $p < 0.001$, multivariate $\eta2 = 0.10$. This indicated that the linear composite of SEL knowledge, learning anxiety and dropout intention at posttest differed for TASSEL intervention and SEL intervention. We also conducted follow-up MANOVA to identify the main effect of intervention type on each variable separately.

For SEL knowledge, from Table 4.15, the Follow-up MANOVA test showed that there was a significant main effect of intervention type, F $(1, 205)$ $= 4.51$, $p < 0.05$, $\eta2 = 0.02$. From table 4.16, we can see that TASSEL intervention had better intervention effect on improving SEL knowledge than SEL intervention. Our result is consistent with previous studies. According to previous literature review, when teachers supported students with competency, students demonstrated educational and developmental benefits, such as better participation, higher level of learning quality, preference for the best challenges, improved internal motivation, higher level of school performance (Guay et al., 2008; Reeve et al., 2004; vansteenkister et al., 2004).

For learning anxiety, from Table 4.17, the Follow-up MANOVA test showed that there was a significant main effect of intervention type, F $(1, 205)$ $= 17.31$, $p < 0.001$, $\eta2 = 0.08$. From Table 4.17, for learning anxiety, we can see that SEL intervention had better intervention effect than TASSEL intervention. This indicated that SEL intervention alone can reduce students' learning anxiety, but TASSEL did not help to reduce learning anxiety, instead, TASSEL increased Chinese rural junior middle school students' learning anxiety.

As Chinese culture is a collectivist culture, which is totally different from the Western individualism culture, like the USA (Triandis et al. , 1988). Chinese students are trained to follow rules and obey rules given by adults since kindergarten (Chang, 2017; Culp, 2020). Under collectivist culture circumstance, children are told not to be independent, not to be excellent in groups, just follow elders, like teachers and parents. Chinese students feel safer and more comfortable to be dependent and have less anxiety when they are in the group. For instance, when the teacher wants to ask a question in class, the students prefer to answer it together. However, if the teacher wants to find a volunteer to answer, everyone will be so nervous, as everyone is worried about giving a wrong answer and will be blamed by the teacher and be laughed at by classmates.

For Chinese students, if you give them authority in class to decide what to do. They may feel confused and do not know what to do. They just want to follow the instruction of their teachers, and they do not enjoy authority given by teachers. Conversely, the authority adds burden and learning anxiety to them. That was why in the TASSEL intervention groups, the learning anxiety did not reduce, but conversely increased. Chinese culture is totally different from American culture. American culture encourages students to get authority in class, and to be independent, to show yourself to others. Hence, from our research, we can see TASSEL intervention was not helpful to reduce learning anxiety based on Chinese collectivism culture background. This result gives us a suggestion that when we applying the Western culture intervention to collectivism culture on particular purposes, we should modify it according to our culture background to make it proper and suitable for our participants.

For dropout intention, from Table 4. 15, the Follow-up MANOVA test showed there was no significant main effect of intervention type, $F (1, 205) = 0.17$, $p > 0.05$, $\eta 2 = 0.00$. From Table 4. 18, for dropout intention, we can see that, there was no significant difference between TASEL and SEL intervention on reducing dropout intention, but when we compare the average score in each group from pretest to posttest, we can see that each group can reduce learning anxiety, which meant both TASSEL and SEL intervention can reduce dropout intention. This proved Strong Kids based intervention is a proper SEL intervention choice for Chinese students to reduce dropout intention.

5.2.3 Research Question 3: Is there significant interaction effect of teacher type (RT vs PT) and intervention type (SEL vs TASSEL) on the combination of SEL knowledge, learning anxiety and dropout intention at posttest?

From Table 4.14, the 2 × 2 MANOVA with posttest showed that there was a significant interaction effect between teacher type and intervention type on the combination of SEL knowledge, learning anxiety and dropout intention at posttest, Wilks' $\Lambda = 0.95$, F (3, 203) $= 3.92$, $p < 0.05$, multivariate $\eta 2 = 0.06$. This indicated that the linear composite of SEL knowledge, learning anxiety and dropout intention differed by the interaction effect of teacher type and intervention type at posttest. We also conducted Follow-up MANOVA to identify the interaction effect between teacher type and intervention type on each variable separately.

For SEL knowledge, from Table 4.15, the Follow-up MANOVA test showed that there was no significant interaction effect of teacher type and intervention type at posttest on SEL knowledge, F (1, 205) $= 2.22$, $p > 0.05$, $\eta 2 = 0.01$. From Figure 4.4, we can see that each group can improve SEL knowledge, consistent with previous research by Skiba (2017) and Gueldner (2007), which also implied that the Strong Kids based intervention is a proper SEL intervention choice for Chinese students.

For learning anxiety, from Table 4.15, the Follow-up MANOVA test showed that there was significant interaction effect of teacher type and intervention type F (1, 205) $= 6.34$, $p < 0.05$, $\eta 2 = 0.03$. From Figure 4.5, we can see that, for learning anxiety, there was significant interaction effect of teacher type and intervention type on learning anxiety, which showed that PT + SEL group had best intervention effect on reducing learning anxiety. Even psychology teachers can not reduce learning anxiety alone, as Chinese students learning anxiety is mostly based on High School Entrance Examination, which mostly refers to regular teachers' help. However, when teacher type and intervention type are mixed, we found that PT + SEL group is the best combination to reduce learning anxiety. This may due to psychology teachers have more knowledge and skills, and SEL intervention is more effective to reduce learning anxiety than TASSEL intervention for Chinese students, so the combination of PT + SEL was most suitable to reduce learning anxiety. This was also consistent with the result of table 4.20, which showed the PT + SEL group reduced learning anxiety by -0.62 score, which was the best reduction of learning anxiety from pretest to posttest.

For dropout intention, from Table 4.15, the Follow-up MANOVA test showed there was significant interaction effect of teacher type and intervention type, F $(1, 205)$ $= 5.11$, $p < 0.05$, $\eta2 = 0.02$. From Figure 4.6, we can see that, for dropout intention, PT + TASSEL group had best intervention effect on reducing dropout intention. This was because TASSEL intervention set up an autonomy support environment to motivate students' inner motivation to keep students staying at school (Guay et al., 2008; Reeve et al., 2004; vansteenkister et al., 2004), and psychology teachers had more psychological knowledge and techniques to help reduce dropout intention at the same time, which worked together to make PT + TASSEL the best combination intervention to reduce dropout intention.

5.2.4   Research Question 4: Is there significant main effect of groups on the combination of SEL knowledge, learning anxiety and dropout intention among four groups from pretest to posttest?

From Table 4.20, we can see that there was significant difference of groups from pretest to posttest score on the combination of SEL knowledge, learning anxiety and dropout intention among four groups from pretest to posttest, Wilks' Λ $= 0.86$, F $(3, 205)$ $= 3.66$, $p < 0.01$, $\eta2 = 0.05$. The main effect of groups indicated that the difference within the four groups on the linear combination of the three dependent variables was different between posttest and pretest. Examinations of the means suggested that this was because groups did not differ on either dependent variable at the time of the pretest (which was consistent with 2×2 factorial MANOVA at pretest level), but they did differ, at the time of the posttest level on all the dependent variables, for each variable difference, we further discussed in 5.2.6.

5.2.5　Research Question 5: Is there significant main effect of time on the combination of SEL knowledge, learning anxiety and dropout intention from pretest to posttest in each group?

From Table 4.20, we can see that there was significant difference of time in each group from pretest to posttest score on the combination of SEL knowledge, learning anxiety and dropout intention from pretest to posttest in each group, Wilks' $\Lambda = 0.74$, F $(3, 205) = 23.25$, $p < 0.01$, $\eta 2 = 0.26$. Examinations of the means suggested that this was due to groups did not differ in each group on either dependent variable at the time of the pretest (which was consistent with our 2×2 factorial MANOVA at pretest level), but they did differ, at the time of the posttest in each group on all the dependent variables.

From Table 4.23, we can see that Follow-up MANOVA revealed that the significant change from pretest to posttest in each group was significant for SEL knowledge, F $(3, 205) = 40.23$, $p < 0.01$, $\eta 2 = 0.16$, learning anxiety, F $(3, 205) = 6.56$, $p < 0.05$, $\eta 2 = 0.03$, as well as dropout intention, F $(3, 205) = 10.51$, $p < 0.01$, $\eta 2 = 0.05$. Hence, Strong Kids curriculum is a proper SEL curriculum for Chinese students.

5.2.6　Research Question 6: Is there significant interaction effect of Time X Group on the combination of SEL knowledge, learning anxiety and dropout intention from pretest to posttest?

From Table 4.22, we can see that there was significant interaction effect of

Time X Group on the combination of SEL knowledge, learning anxiety and dropout intention from pretest to posttest, Wilks' $\Lambda = 0.87$, F (3, 205) $= 3.11$, $p < 0.01$, $\eta 2 = 0.04$.

We conducted post hoc test to further explore the Time × Group interaction effect on each dependent variable. From post hoc test, we found that, for SEL knowledge, PT + TASSEL intervention group had significantly higher score than RT + SEL intervention group from pretest to posttest (mean difference $= 1.29$, $p < 0.05$), which meant that PT + TASSEL intervention group was the best choice at increasing SEL knowledge. For dropout intention, PT + TASSEL intervention group had significantly lower score than RT + TASSEL group from pretest to posttest (mean difference $= -0.61$, $p < 0.01$), which also meant that PT + TASSEL intervention group was the best choice to reduce dropout intention. However, for learning anxiety, there was no significant difference in four groups from pretest to posttest.

5.2.7 Research Question 7: Is the present intervention effective to reduce rural junior middle school students' learning anxiety percentage from pretest to posttest?

For learning anxiety rate, our research result was similar with previous studies, which had found junior middle school student's learning anxiety rate as high as 66 percent in rural China (Wang et al. , 2015).

From Table 4.23 and Figure 4.10, we can see that, among the four groups, RT + SEL group and PT + SEL group had the ability to reduce rural junior middle school students' learning anxiety percentage by 3.9 percent and 8 percent separately, and these two groups reduced more than 2.3 percent of learning anxiety, which was reported by Wang (2016) intervention effect. As a result, we can see that the present study was effective to reduce rural junior middle school students' learning anxiety percentage from pretest to posttest, especially with RT + SEL group and PT + SEL group interventions.

Furthermore, when we compared RT + SEL group and PT + SEL group, we can see that PT + SEL group has the best intervention effect to reduce learning anxiety. SEL intervention is a proper choice to reduce learning anxiety, as in Chinese collectivism culture, students did not like to be independent, because independence would add psychological burden to them. Although psychology teachers can not reduce learning anxiety alone, when psychology teachers mixed with SEL intervention, the knowledge and skill of psychology teachers also have better effect to help reduce learning anxiety, compared to regular teachers mixed with SEL intervention. Hence, PT + SEL group had the best intervention effect, which should be a good choice to reduce learning anxiety for Chinese students.

5. 2. 8　Research Question 8: Is the present intervention effective to reduce rural junior middle school students' dropout intention percentage from pretest to posttest?

From Table 4. 24 and Figure 11, we can see that RT + SEL intervention group reduced dropout intention by 7. 9 percent, RT + TASSEL intervention group reduced dropout intention by 14. 5 percent, PT + SEL intervention group reduced dropout intention by 18. 7 percent, PT + TASSEL intervention group reduced dropout intention by 39. 6 percent. Among the four groups had the ability to reduce rural junior middle school students' dropout intention percentage, and each group reduced more than 1. 6 percent dropout intention, which was reported by Wang (2016) intervention effect, which meant that our Strong Kids based SEL interventions were effective to reduce rural junior middle school students' dropout intention percentage from pretest to posttest. From Table 4. 24, we can deduce that PT + TASSEL intervention group had reduced highest dropout intention percentage in the current study. This was due to psychology teachers had more knowledge and technique to implement psychological intervention, and at the same time, TASSEL intervention set up a friendly and cozy circumstance for students to foster inner motivation by satisfying their relatedness for study at school and reduced dropout intention. In this case, our best suggestion for reducing dropout intention intervention is PT + TASSEL, which can be widely applied in Chinese rural junior middle school.

5. 3 Implication of the Findings

The findings and critical review of the literature are thought to have made constructive contribution to the theory and its practices in real life classroom. This part of the chapter concentrated on the theoretical and practical significances. The section below discussed in detail the methodological and instrumentation aspects as major theoretical implications.

5. 3. 1   Theoretical Implications

5. 3. 1. 1   Methodology

Firstly, Strong Kids was the first time to be used as a SEL intervention in China to reduce dropout intention and learning anxiety which was implemented as rural junior middle school students' compulsory psychological well-being course, and it was modified according to Chinese culture, so it can set an example to use Strong Kids based curriculum as compulsory psychological well-being course for Chinese rural junior middle school students.

Secondly, based on how to deliver Strong Kids curriculum more effectively, this was the first attempt to integrate teacher autonomy supportive intervention type to Strong Kids curriculum. As teacher autonomy supportive instructions has been proven to be effective to reduce learning anxiety and dropout rate (Hardre & Reeve, 2003). Hence, teacher autonomy supportive Strong Kids curriculum was further modified to explore if teacher autonomy supportive instructions would improve the effect of SEL intervention, compared with the effect of original Strong Kids intervention alone on reducing learning anxiety and dropout intention.

Based on our discussion about the intervention effect on students' SEL knowledge, learning anxiety and dropout intention, compare teacher autonomy supportive Strong Kids intervention with Strong Kids intervention, we concluded that teacher autonomy supportive Strong Kids intervention was better at improving SEL knowledge and reducing dropout intention, which indicated that teacher autonomy supportive Strong Kids intervention was better than Strong Kids intervention to increase SEL knowledge and reduce dropout intention for rural junior middle school students in rural China. As a result, we suggest teacher autonomy supportive Strong Kids intervention can be applied as a suitable intervention to reduce rural junior middle school students' dropout intention. However, for learning anxiety, based on Chinese collectivism culture background, it was better to choose Strong Kids intervention, other than teacher autonomy supportive Strong Kids intervention, as students felt more comfortable in a less teacher autonomy supportive but dependent environment to study.

Thirdly, in the present research, teacher selection is another theoretical implementation. According to literature reviews, teachers of any kind can implement SEL intervention. However, in the current research, we had doubts about previous statement about teacher selection and compared the effect of psychology teacher with regular teacher on our dependent variables.

From our intervention effect, we can see that psychology teacher was better than regular teacher at improving SEL knowledge and reducing dropout intention, which indicated psychology teacher was better than regular teacher for implementing Strong Kids based intervention. As a result, we suggest that psychology teacher should be chosen to implement SEL and TASSEL intervention.

When the intervention methods and teacher types were combined, there were four different intervention groups, and these four groups had different interaction effects on our three dependent variables. According to these four groups, teacher autonomy supportive Strong Kids intervention group with psychology teacher had the best intervention effect on SEL knowledge and dropout intention, which implied that teacher autonomy supportive Strong Kids intervention group with psychology teacher was the best combination for improving SEL knowledge and reducing psychological health problem for rural junior middle school students. Nevertheless, for learning anxiety, the psychological teacher with Strong Kids based SEL intervention group has the best intervention effect.

5. 3. 1. 2   Validation of the Instruments

Another critical theoretical implication of the current study was the validation of the instruments utilized in measuring SEL knowledge, dropout intention. Particularly, this was the first time when these instruments were used with Chinese rural junior middle school students in middle education settings. The process of the instruments' validity was established by conducting the exploratory factor analysis (EFA) technique in SPSS (version 25.0). Cronbach's alpha was performed to check the reliability of the instruments in this research. The results revealed that the two scales, with slight adaptations, were confirmed in terms of their reliability and validity with Chinese rural junior middle school students in elementary education settings.

5. 3. 2   Practical Implications

Concerning the practical implications, the obtained findings in current research have made substantial contributions in the Chinese middle educational settings. The following sections explain each practical contribution in details.

5. 3. 2. 1   The development of TASSEL intervention

In the current study, our predominant practical contribution is the development of TASSEL intervention. As original SEL intervention needs to add teacher autonomy supportive instructions to improve students' engagement to get the expected school outcomes, such as improving SEL knowledge and reducing learning anxiety and dropout. Hence, we carefully analyzed the teacher autonomy supportive instructions and then we discussed with Chinese psychologists and school counseling teachers in China to choose the proper six teacher autonomy supportive instructions to add to the original SEL intervention, and after that we had a pilot experiment to check our TASSEL model and had some revisions after the pilot experiment, such as we changed our warm-up activities from hypnotic activities to word games, as the previous activities did not work well on the rural junior middle school students in China. We also explained some keywords according to Chinese culture to assist understanding of their meanings for Chinese students. After all of our experts agreed with our revision of TASSEL intervention, we had developed our final version of TASSEL intervention.

5.3.2.2　TASSEL intervention as a compulsory psychological well-being class which can be replicated in other rural junior middle schools in China

In this research, we implemented TASSEL intervention as a compulsory psychological well-being class for rural junior middle school students. As there is no particular psychological well-being class curriculum in rural middle high schools in China, many school psychology teachers do not know what and how to teach psychological well-being class. In this case, TASSEL intervention gives other rural junior middle schools an example about what and how to teach in psychological well-being class. Furthermore, TASSEL intervention also has teacher training about how to teach. TASSEL intervention includes a 2-day training about what is TASSEL, how to implement TASSEL, and prepares all the slides and fidelity checklists for teachers and also there is a pacing guide by researcher which will guide the teachers to implement the TASSEL intervention, and will answer any question when teachers have problems in implementation.

5.3.2.3　TASSEL intervention assist to foster high-educated citizens and maintain national stability by reducing students' dropout intention.

When the TASSEL intervention works, the rural junior middle school students' dropout reduces. Therefore, it will help more rural junior middle students continue their study at rural junior middle school and have more chance to enter high school or even college or university. In this way, it will reduce the low-educated citizens from the countryside. When more and more citizens are high-educated, it will reduce the consumption of social wealth of low-educated citizens, while increasing the value of individual labor force and maintain national stability by reducing disparities between cities and counties.

5.3.2.4   To Advice Educational Policy Makers to Pay Attention to the Cultivation of Students' Emotional Intelligence and Implement TASSEL Intervention in Rural Junior Middle School in China

Goleman (2000) declared that individuals' success 15 percent depends on Intelligence Quotient (IQ), 85 percent depends on Emotional Intelligence (EI). When the TASSEL intervention works, it helps to improve the citizens' emotional intelligence, and it will enhance their adaptive and competitive techniques, which will help them to survive in their future life and benefit the whole society. Hence, this study gives strong advice for Chinese educational policemakers to pay more attention to the cultivation of students' emotional intelligence and implement TASSEL intervention as a compulsory psychological well-being class, and hire psychological teachers to implement TASSEL intervention.

5.4   Limitation

Although there are many benefits of Strong Kids based intervention in the current study, there are also some limitations, which are discussed below.

5.4.1   Lack of True Experimental Design

The most effective way to evaluate the effect of educational intervention is to use real experimental design. However, it was impossible to execute a randomized treatment-control experimental design. The quasi-experimental design is considered to be very close to the pure experimental design, and its findings are considered reliable if the design includes all preventive measures (Ary et al., 2005). However, due to various internal and external validity threats, the design has its limitations. If these threats are not controlled, the results can be jeopardized (Gay & Airasian, 2003). The third chapter of this study explained in detail the procedures adopted to control these threats. However, strictly controlling these menaces is like creating laboratory conditions and deteriorating quasi-experimental designs. Classroom intervention, without school and neighbourhood context, lacks a broader ecological perspective to understand the program effect. Therefore, potential threats that may be associated with the design of such studies must be considered before replicating this study.

5.4.2   Lack of Multiple Evaluations

In the current study, students' social emotional knowledge and problem behaviors were only measured by student self-reports. There were no evaluations from teachers and parents. We did not know how teachers evaluate the changes of students and how parents evaluated their children at home (Erin et al., 2020). If we can get multiple evaluations, it will give us a broader understanding of intervention effect. Furthermore, we only evaluated the project based on the social knowledge and problem behaviors of the participants. We did not include other variables, like academic achievement, etc. (Agnes, et al., 2014).

5.4.3   Lack of Longitudinal Intervention

Durlak et al. (2016) identified that there was a big challenge to conduct SEL intervention like Strong Kids for a continuous period of time. There is a research gap to conduct longitudinal study, especially for Strong Kids series studies. Each of the existing studies to investigate the participants for only one intervention cycle. Until now, there is no study which focuses on students' long-time intervention outcome after several years' exposure to the intervention. It may be very interesting to evaluate how students' social-emotional competency and academic outcomes will change after several years' intervention. In our research, the intervention time lasted only three months without follow-up assessments. It cannot determine the extent of the beneficial impact over time. Furthermore, in this study, we only used dropout intention, instead of real dropout rate as dependent variable. Ideally, it's better to include both dropout intention and real dropout rate by a longitudinal study.

5.4.4 Lack of Survey about Intervention Needs from Teachers before Intervention and Students' Opinion after Intervention

In the present research, we do not ask teachers in advance if their students need SEL intervention. It is better for teachers to recognize the necessity and value of the intervention and to buy-in such a program and implement for their students. If the teachers are more interested in the intervention, they will be more enthusiastic and serious when they deliver the intervention, which will improve the intervention effect. Secondly, to improve the effect of Strong Kids intervention, it also needs to have a survey on students, like how they view the Strong Kids curriculum they learned for 12 weeks, what are participants' suggestions for improving the program.

5.5 Future Research Recommendation

Based on the limitations of this study, we have some recommendations for future research. The following are details of the suggestions for future research.

5.5.1 Multiple Evaluations

Future researchers can investigate the change in distinct circumstances, such as family environment to school scene. In the future, the participation of multiple raters, such as classroom observation, teacher report and parents report, will be more objective (Erin et al., 2020). Approaching research on the effect of SEL projects should also include measures that center on a wide range of positive assets, as this may be a way to test the effects of Strong Kids. If future research can also measure participants' academic performance, it will be more beneficial. As Chinese culture attaches great importance to learning achievement, if the research can justify that SEL intervention has the capacity to enhance social emotional technique and academic performance in Chinese circumstance, the public will pay more attention to the benefits of SEL intervention (Wong et al., 2014). Furthermore, whether students' relationships with teachers and classmates can be improved according to the participation in the SEL project, can be considered as future research area.

5.5.2　Longitudinal Intervention Study

In order to track the development of junior middle school students from Grade 7 to Grade 9, a pretest-posttest and extended posttest design can effectively observe the three-year period changes. This will not only provide a long-term perspective, but will also have great value compared with the long-term program evaluated by Taylor et al. (2017). Furthermore, this may also include bringing it into student stratified interventions at all levels. Using students' social techniques investigation as a screening tool, students can be divided into groups according to their techniques defects, and require junior middle school counselors to apply Strong Kids as part of retelling to improve the techniques of students who need more repetition to succeed. Since some of the students perhaps require more support than a Strong Kids as Tier Ⅰ intervention, future research can look at increasing Tier Ⅱ and Tier Ⅲ interventions to improve student performance.

5.5.3　Investigating Teachers' and Students' Views on SEL Intervention

As Durlak et al. (2016) suggested, greater teacher autonomy support can improve results through higher implementation loyalty, thus bringing stronger results to students. In future research, researchers should first have a survey about teachers to investigate if they believe their students need SEL intervention.

If teachers agree, this indicates they will be more cooperative and will help improve the intervention effect. Furthermore, students should also be investigated after intervention to identify how they think about the intervention and what suggestions for future implementation of such an intervention.

5. 6   Conclusion

Since 2001, the dropout rate of rural junior middle school in China was very high because of the merger program, and "reduce dropout" has become the urgent theme of MoE in China. Wang, et al. (2016) discovered that high dropout of rural junior middle school students was strongly linked to mental health problem, especially learning anxiety. Hence, it was necessary to implement some psychological health program to reduce mental health problem and dropout in rural junior middle school. CASEL (2017) found that SEL intervention is a positive intervention program which can help weaken psychological health problem and reduce dropout. Wang (2015) implemented SEL intervention based on self-compiled SEL curriculum to reduce rural junior middle school students' learning anxiety and dropout intention. However, the effect of reducing learning anxiety was 2. 3 percent and dropout rate was 1. 6 percent, which had a far distance with the real leaning anxiety of 66 percent and dropout rate of 27 percent.

Based on the literature review, there was a big gap to improve the intervention effect of reducing learning anxiety percentage and dropout intention percentage among rural junior middle school to reduce the number of students who are going to dropout of school. There were many factors which affect the effect of an intervention, like what curriculum to choose, what kind of teacher to choose, what intervention type to choose. As present existing SEL intervention curriculums were all complicated and expensive to implement, which was not suitable for rural junior middle school. However, Strong Kids curriculum, which was cost-effective, easy to implement, and had been proven to reduce learning anxiety and dropout (Merrell, 2008), was selected as target SEL course for this study.

Furthermore, compared to previous research to choose any kind of teacher to deliver SEL intervention, in the present research, psychology teacher and regular teacher were both chosen to compare the effect of teacher type on reducing learning anxiety and dropout intention.

When the intervention type was concerned, as teacher autonomy support had been proven to creat a friendly environment for students to study and can help reduce learning anxiety and dropout rate. As a result, teacher autonomy support instructions were added to Strong Kids curriculum to compare the effect of reducing learning anxiety and dropout intention.

There were four groups of combination based on teacher types and intervention types. The main objective of this study was to find the better match of teacher type and intervention type to implement Strong Kids intervention for reducing rural junior middle school students' learning anxiety and dropout intention. Our hypothesis was that teacher autonomy supportive Strong Kids intervention implemented by psychology teacher would have the best intervention effect on reducing learning anxiety and dropout intention.

This study aimed to make up for a few research gaps discovered in former Strong Kids studies. Firstly, there was no SEL intervention like Strong Kids curriculum in China at present, so this research was the first time to use Strong Kids curriculum intervention in China to investigate its culture adaptation. Secondly, although there were some SEL interventions in China to reduce learning anxiety and dropout intention, but the effect was not strong enough. There was a big space to improve the intervention effect. Thirdly, how to implement Strong Kids intervention and what kind of teacher would be better at implementing Strong Kids intervention has not been decided yet. Hence, in this research, a 2 × 2 quasi-factorial experiment design (2 intervention types, teacher autonomy supportive SEL intervention and SEL curriculum; 2 teacher types, psychology teacher and regular teacher) was applied to find the best combination of intervention type and teacher type to deliver Strong Kids curriculum to improve SEL knowledge, reduce learning anxiety and dropout intention.

The results appeared promising: The 12-session teacher autonomy supportive

Strong Kids intervention with psychology teacher was best at improving SEL knowledge and reducing dropout intention. Teacher autonomy supportive SEL intervention can set a friendly environment to satisfy students' relatedness and competence need, which helped students had more confidence and interest to study and stay at school. As a result, it increased students' SEL knowledge and reduced dropout intention. As demonstrated in the result and discussion part, psychology teachers who had more technique and knowledge in psychology were more suitable to implement SEL intervention. As a result, teacher autonomy supportive SEL intervention with psychology teacher intervention should be recommended as a cost-effective and easy way to implement course for rural junior middle school in China, which is one of the effactive solutions to reduce dropout in rural junior middle school for MoE of China.

However, for learning anxiety, the result was different and unique. According to our research result, we found that teacher autonomy supportive instruction gave students more psychological burden in class due to Chinese collectivism culture. In Chinese collectivism culture, students usually like to study together, and they do not like to be independent as independence which may give them more chance to make mistakes and more likely to be negatively judged by peers. As a result, to reduce learning anxiety, SEL intervention is better than TASSEL intervention. As demonstrated in the result and discussion part, to psychology teachers who have more technique and knowledge in psychology, they are more suitable to implement SEL intervention. Hence, for learning anxiety, the more available combination group is PT + SET group.

Appendix A: Strong Kids Sample Lesson

Lesson 1: About Strong Kids

Introduction

Today, we will begin a new curriculum called Strong Kids. In this curriculum, we will discuss how to understand our emotions and the emotions of others. We will also discuss how to solve problems, how to set goals, and how to think in a way that helps us in life. We will meet once a week for about 45 minutes. You will learn important new techniques that will help you work well with others and make good choices. Everyone needs to be healthy—emotionally and physically. This curriculum will help you learn techniques that you may use to be emotionally healthy throughout your life.

Procedure

· Introduction to the Topics Covered in the Curriculum

During this 12-lesson curriculum, we will discuss these topics (refer to the handout, supplement 1. 1). Today's lesson will help us to understand our goals for Strong Kids. Other lessons will help us learn to identify our emotions and good ways to express them; to talk about our anger and give us good ways to deal with it; to notice and better understand other people's feelings; and to think in ways that help us in life. We will also learn how to solve people's problems and conflicts, and how to relax, keep active, and achieve our goals.

· Awareness or Disclaimer Statement: Students with Serious Problems

The Strong Kids curriculum focused on life techniques and might not be enough to help for students experiencing a large amount of depression or anxiety. If you feel you are experiencing these issues or you know someone who might, see me so that we can support you in getting the help you need.

· Defining Behavior Expectations

During our curriculum, you may be asked to share stories about when you felt a strong emotion, such as anger, or when you've had a problem. You can raise your hand when you have a story to share. When someone is sharing a story, we are respectful by listening quietly while they are talking. Also, because stories might be personal, they will just stay in the class; this is called confidentiality, and it is an important part of being respectful during Strong Kids. If you decide that you no longer want to share your story or if you begin to feel uncomfortable, you may stop at any time. If you do not feel comfortable sharing your story with the whole group but you feel like you want to talk to someone, please speak to me after class.

We also need to be safe and responsible during Strong Kids. Being safe during our curriculum means keeping our hands and feet to ourselves. Being responsible during our curriculum means completing your teamwork assignments and raising your hand to ask questions when you don't understand something.

· Closure

Today, we talked about Strong Kids, our new curriculum. For the next 11 weeks, we will learn about our feelings, learning how to deal with them, and learning other important life techniques. During this time, we need to remember to be safe, respectful and responsible, just like during any other class or activity at school.

· Teamwork Handout (Supplement 1.3)

Appendix B: Teacher Autonomy Supportive Strong Kids Modification Lesson Outlines

Lesson 1: About Strong Kids

Ⅰ. Start session

Allow students to choose their seats and sit with their friends.

Ⅱ. Structure session

Tell students there are five steps in this lesson.

Step 1: Introduce the Strong Kids Curriculum outline.

Step 2: Introduce the class rules for students to obey.

Step 3: Introduce the keywords in this lesson.

Step 4: Personal experience sharing.

Step 5: Facial expression guessing game (teamwork).

Ⅲ. Ration for lesson 1

Lesson 1 is to inform students with Strong Kids curriculum outline to help students have a main idea of what will be learned this semester, inform students class rules to make sure students will be engaged during class and to keep secret for the intervention content. Facial expression guessing game is an interesting game to help students enjoy the intervention and to be aware of the variety of facial expressions and how people express complex facial expressions on certain circumstances.

IV. Teaching activities

Activity 1: Warm up (Personal experience sharing session)

Ask students to recall a moment when they feel one kind or several kinds of emotions. Use appendix 1. 7 of Strong Kids book to answer these questions and then share in class.

Activity 2: Introduce the Strong Kids Curriculum outline

Use appendix 1. 4 for introducing Strong Kids Curriculum outline.

Activity 3: Introduce the class rules for students to obey

Use appendix 1. 2 for instructing class rules.

Activity 4: Introduce the keywords in this lesson

Use appendix 1. 5 for teaching keywords.

Activity 5: Facial expression guessing game (teamwork)

Use appendix 1. 6, and ask one volunteer student who is good at acting to act in front of class and other students to guess what facial emotion the volunteer expresses.

Lesson 2: Understanding Your Feelings 1

I. Start session

Allow students to choose their seats and sit with their friends.

II. Structure session

There are three steps in this lesson.

Step 1: Introduce and explain the keywords.

Step 2: A. Develop the ability to identify physical feelings that occur with emotions.

B. Identify emotions on a continuum from comfortable to uncomfortable.

C. Measure the intensity of emotions.

Step 3: Skill Practice—Identify and measure your emotions

Ⅲ. Ration for lesson 2

Lesson 2 is aimed at helping students develop the ability to identify physical feelings that occur with emotions, and use emotion volume slider to help students to measure their own emotion status, and learn how to control their emotion by identifying their physical feelings.

Ⅳ. Teaching activities

Activity 1: Warm up activity (personal experience sharing session)

Ask students to recall a moment when they feel one kind or several kinds of emotions. Use appendix 1. 7 to answer these questions and then share them in class.

Activity 2: Keywords learning

Use appendix 2. 2 for keywords learning.

Activity 3: Listen and identify emotions from music

Lecturer plays different kinds of music (depressed, sad, calm, happy, excited) on the computer, and ask students to tell the feelings when they hear each piece of music.

Activity 4: Identify physical feelings that occur with emotions

Activity 5: Measure the intensity of emotions

Show a horror scene from a movie, and ask students to measure how scared they are by it. Use appendix 2. 4 emotion volume slider.

Activity 6: Skill practice (teamwork) —Identify and measure your emotions

Use appendix 2. 5. Ask students to work in pairs, write down their own answers first, and then exchange their answers with their partners.

Lesson 3: Understanding Your Feelings 2

Ⅰ. Start session

Allow students to choose their seats and sit with their friends.

Ⅱ. Structure session

There are three steps in this lesson.

Step 1: Introduce and explain the keywords.

Step 2: A. Identify thoughts and behaviors that occur with emotions.

B. Identify your emotion with helpful or unhelpful way of communication under certain background.

Step 3: Skill Practice—how to express your emotions with helpful ways in certain circumstances.

Ⅲ. Ration for lesson 3

Lesson 3 is aimed at helping students acknowledge that emotion is connected with their thoughts and behaviors, and they can change their emotions when they change their thoughts and behaviors, and teach students to master the helpful ways to express their emotions to have good relationships with others and to behave properly with emotions and behaviors in any given circumstance.

Ⅳ. Teaching activities

Activity 1: Warm up activity (storytelling and personal experience sharing)

A: Storytelling

The teacher will tell the story of "crying as old granny and laughing as old granny" to ask students to think about how people can change their mood by change their thoughts and behaviors.

B: Students, personal experience sharing

Ask students to share a similar story in their own life.

Activity 2: Keywords learning

Use appendix 3. 2 for keywords learning.

Activity 3: Identify thoughts and behaviors that occur with emotions.

Use appendix 3. 4 to write down your emotions, thoughts, behaviors under each circumstance.

Activity 4: Identify your emotion with helpful or unhelpful way of expression under certain background.

Use appendix 3. 5 to identify each situation, to check if it is a helpful or unhelpful way to express emotions.

Activity 5: Skill practice (teamwork) —use proper thoughts and behaviors to express your emotion in a particular situation.

Ask students to write down how they feel and what they will think and do when they will have examination tomorrow and there is a world cup football show on TV tonight.

Lesson 4: Understanding Other People's Feelings

Ⅰ. Start session

Allow students to choose their seats and sit with their friends.

Ⅱ. Structure session

There are three steps in this lesson.

Step 1: Introduce and explain the keywords.

Step 2: A. Use context to understand other people's feeling.

B. Identify other people's feelings.

Step 3: Skill Practice—How to be a considerable person by taking other people's seat?

Ⅲ. Ration for lesson 4

Lesson 4 is aimed at helping students to take others' seat to cultivate empathy by identifying and considering others' situations and emotions.

Ⅳ. Teaching activities

Activity 1: Warm-up activity (storytelling and personal experience sharing)

A: Story telling

The teacher will share a story why a little girl in kindergarten always wears her socks during sleeping time.

B: Students, personal experience sharing

Ask students to share a similar story in their own life, whether to help others or been helped by others.

Activity 2: Keywords learning

Use appendix 4. 1 for keywords learning.

Activity 3: Role-play (teamwork)

Allocate students to pairs. Ask each pair of students to play the role of parent and child, and discuss the problem of their nervous relationship in adolescent period.

Activity 4: Identify other people's feelings.

Use appendix 4. 2 to teach students how to identify other people's feelings.

Activity 5: Skill practice—How to be a considerable person by taking other people's seat?

Use appendix 4. 4. Allocate students to pairs, and ask each pair of students to practice empathy skills.

Lesson 5: Dealing with Anger

I. Start session

Allow students to choose their seats and sit with their friends.

II. Structure session

There are three steps in this lesson.

Step 1: Introduce and explain the keywords.

Step 2: A. Identify the triggers of anger, understand anger model.

B. Anger control strategy

Step 3: Skill practice—Use anger control strategy to handle your anger.

III. Ration for lesson 5

Lesson 5 is aimed at teaching students how to identify the reasons that make them get angry, and understand the anger model, which tells the procedure of emotion, behavior and result of anger, and how to manage their anger proactively during the thinking and emotion periods before taking real actions.

IV. Teaching activities

Activity 1: Warm-up activity (storytelling and personal experience sharing)

When is your most anger moment in your life? Why did you get so angry and what happened with your anger?

Activity 2: Keywords learning

Use appendix 5. 1 for keywords learning.

Activity 3: Identify the triggers of anger and understand anger model.

Use appendix 5.5 to identify your anger trigger, learn the process of anger model, and know that we can control our anger during the emotion reaction and action sections. If we think positively, the result will be positive.

Activity 4: How to positively control our anger?

Use appendix 5.7 to master the techniques to positively control your anger. Always be calm down, and consider things and people positively to help lead things to a positive way and result.

Activity 5: Skill practice (teamwork) —use anger control worksheet to practice how to control your anger in a positive way.

Use appendix 5.8. Ask students to discuss in pairs, write down their anger and select a positive anger control method to think and behave positively to solve their anger.

Lesson 6: Clear Thinking 1

Ⅰ. Start session

Allow students to choose their seats and sit with their friends.

Ⅱ. Structure session

There are three steps in this lesson.

Step 1: Introduce and explain the keywords.

Step 2: A. Understand the influence of thoughts on emotions and behaviors, and develop an awareness of their own thoughts.

B. Identify common thinking traps that affect behaviors, thoughts and emotions.

Step 3: Skill practice—Identify common thinking traps that affect behaviors, thoughts and emotions.

Ⅲ. Ration for lesson 6

Lesson 6 is aimed at teaching students to understand the influence of thoughts on emotions and behaviors and identify thinking traps during their thinking process.

If students can be aware of their thoughts and identify their thinking traps, they will think wisely and change their mood and behavior by thinking wisely.

IV. Teaching activities

Activity 1: Warm-up activity (personal experience sharing)

Ask students to tell about one of their failure experiences in their life, and ask students to recall what benefits they got from their failure. Have they ever thought about the benefits before? (A blessing in disguise.)

Activity 2: Keywords learning

Use appendix 6.3 for keywords learning.

Activity 3: Understand the influence of thoughts on emotions and behaviors, and develop an awareness of their own thoughts.

Use appendix 6.1, 6.2, and 6.4 to understand the influence of thoughts on emotions and behaviors, and to develop an awareness of their own thoughts; write your own thoughts, feelings and behaviors when you see appendix 6.1.

Activity 4: Identify common thinking traps that affect behavior, thoughts and emotions.

Use appendix 6.5, 6.6 and 6.7 to identify common thinking traps that affect behavior, thoughts and emotions.

Activity 5: Skill practice (teamwork) —practice identifying common thinking traps that affect behavior, thoughts and emotions.

Use appendix 6.8. Ask students to work in pairs and write down, under some previous experienced circumstance, how they felt, their emotional state, their thoughts, and any thinking traps they encountered?

Lesson 7: Clear Thinking 2

I. Start session

Allow students to choose their seats and sit with their friends.

II. Structure session

There are three steps in this lesson.

Step 1：Introduce and explain the keywords.

Step 2：A. Finding out evidence of thinking trap.

B. Learn techniques to reframe thinking traps.

Step 3：Skill practice—Apply techniques to find evidence of thinking traps and reframe thinking traps.

Ⅲ. Ration for lesson 7

Lesson 7 is aimed at helping students develop the knowledge and skill to find the evidence of their thinking traps and try to reframe of their thinking with healthy thought patterns. Reframe the thinking trap in a positive way can help students promote resilience and social and emotional growth.

Ⅳ. Teaching activities

Activity 1：Warm-up activity (personal experience sharing)

A. Use appendix 7.6 to ask students：Which white circle is bigger? Are they the same size? But why the first white circle looks bigger than the second one? (Optical illusion)

B. Ask students to share some experiences they made mistake in similar situations as example above and why it happened.

Activity 2：Keywords learning

Use appendix 7.3 for keywords learning.

Activity 3：Finding out evidence of thinking trap.

Use appendix 7.5 and 7.7 to find out evidence of thinking trap.

Activity 4：Learn techniques to reframe thinking traps.

Use appendix 7.1 and 7.8 to identify common thinking traps.

Activity 5：Skill practice (teamwork) —Apply techniques to find evidence of thinking traps and reframe thinking trap.

Use appendix 7.9, ask students to work in pairs, write down under some previous experienced circumstances, what thinking trap did they face, what evidence did they find, and how to reframe their thinking trap in a positive way to create a clear and clever thinking?

Lesson 8: Solving People's Problems

I. Start session

Allow students to choose their seats and sit with their friends.

II. Structure session

There are three steps in this lesson.

Step 1: Introduce and explain the keywords.

Step 2: A. What can we do when we face with conflict?

B. Identify the steps of a problem-solving model to resolve conflicts.

Step3: Skill practice—Apply the steps of a problem-solving model to resolve conflicts.

III. Ration for lesson 8

Lesson 8 provides students with ways to have healthy, positive relationships with others by making responsible, respectful and realistic decisions when confronted with a social conflict.

IV. Teaching activities

Activity 1: Warm-up activity (personal experience sharing)

Ask students to share their experience of social conflicts with others and how they solved their conflicts. Discuss whether their ways of solving conflict were healthy, positive and realistic or not.

Activity 2: Keywords learning

Use appendix 8.2 for keywords learning.

Activity 3: What can we do when we face with conflicts?

Use appendix 8.3 to learn how to solve conflicts with healthy, positive and realistic strategies.

Activity 4: Identify the steps of a problem-solving model to resolve conflicts.

Use appendix 8.4 to identify the steps of a problem-solving model to resolve conflicts.

Activity 5: Skill practice (teamwork) —Apply the steps of a problem-solving model to resolve conflicts.

Use appendix 8. 5. Ask students to work in pairs, write down their conflicts and use the four steps to resolve their conflicts.

Lesson 9: Letting Go of Stress

Ⅰ. Start session

Allow students to choose their seats and sit with their friends.

Ⅱ. Structure session

There are three steps in this lesson.

Step 1: Introduce and explain the keywords.

Step 2: A. Identify stress symptoms under example situations.

B. Identify personal triggers and stress.

Step 3: Skill practice—Let your stress go.

Ⅲ. Ration for lesson 9

Lesson 9 provides students with the skills to understand the different kinds of stress and ways to proactively cope with stress.

Ⅳ. Teaching activities

Activity 1: Warm-up activity (personal experience sharing)

Ask students to share their most stressful experience at present, and explain how they deal with their stress and what the result will be.

Activity 2: Keywords learning

Use appendix 9. 2 for keywords learning.

Activity 3: Identify stress symptoms under example situations.

Use appendix 9. 3 to identify the physical, emotional, behavioral stress symptoms in example situations.

Activity 4: Identify personal triggers and stress.

Use appendix 9. 4 to identify personal triggers and stress.

Activity 5: Skill practice (teamwork) —Let your stress go.

Use appendix 9. 5. Ask students to work in pairs, write down their stress, and learn how to let stress go by choosing the proper stress solving method.

Lesson 10: Positive Living

I. Start session

Allow students to choose their seats and sit with their friends.

II. Structure session

There are three steps in this lesson.

Step 1: Introduce and explain the keywords.

Step 2: A. positive living activities.

          B. Weekdays and weekend good habits.

Step 3: Skill practice—how to foster good habits?

III. Ration for lesson 10

Lesson 10 helps the students know what good activities are and what good habits are, and how to foster good habits, as good habits will keep you in a good physical and psychological health status and will make you more resilient.

IV. Teaching activities

Activity 1: Warm-up activity (personal experience sharing)

Ask students to share their experience of daily life activities and if they can identify what are good activities, what are bad activities.

Activity 2: Keywords learning

Use appendix 10. 1 for keywords learning.

Activity 3: Positive living activities

Use appendix 10. 2 to know the good activities.

Activity 4: Weekdays and weekend good habits

Use appendix 10. 3, 10. 4, 10. 5, and 10. 6 to identify good habits for weekdays and weekends.

Activity 5: Skill practice (teamwork) —Positive living.

Use appendix 10. 7. Ask students to work in pairs, write down their activity plan for positive living for one week and share with their partner.

Lesson 11: Creating Strong and Smart Goals

Ⅰ. Start session

Allow students to choose their seats and sit with their friends.

Ⅱ. Structure session

There are three steps in this lesson.

Step 1: Introduce and explain the keywords.

Step 2: A. Understand the smart goals and 5 healthy living domains.

B. Understand examples and non-examples of setting goals and set up your own goals in 5 healthy living domains.

Step 3: Skill practice—how to apply smart goals to set up your goal to finish junior middle school in the following year?

Ⅲ. Ration for lesson 11

Lesson 11 teaches students the skill of goal setting and increasing positive activity as a mean to a healthy life, especially to their junior middle boarding school life.

Ⅳ. Teaching activities

Activity 1: Warm-up activity (personal experience sharing)

Ask students to share their experience of their goal and what they had done to achieve their goal. How is the result?

Activity 2: Keywords learning

Use appendix 11.2 for keywords learning.

Activity 3: Understand the smart goals.

Use appendix 11.3 and 11.5 to teach students what are smart goals, and what are the 5 healthy living domains.

Activity 4: Understand examples and non-examples of setting goals and set up your own smart goals in 5 healthy living domains.

Use appendix 11.3 and 11.4 to understand the examples and non-examples of setting goals and set up your own goals in 5 healthy living domains with examples of smart goals.

Activity 5: Skill practice (teamwork) —Positive living

Use appendix 11.7. Ask students to work in pairs and write down their plan to finish junior middle school in the following year by setting up 5 healthy living domains with smart goals and share with each other.

Lesson 12: Build Your Social Support Network

I . Start session

Allow students to choose their seats and sit with their friends.

II . Structure session

There are three steps in this lesson.

Step 1: Strong Kids Lesson Review

Step 2: A. Enhance an understanding of resilience to school and life success.

B. Develop an awareness of social support system.

Step 3: Skill practice—how to use your social support networks to help you finish your junior middle school study?

III . Ration for lesson 12

Lesson 12 is to help students reverse the previous lessons and enhance an understanding of resilience to school and life, and teach students how to find their social support system to support them to finish their junior middle school study.

IV. Teaching activities

Activity 1: Warm-up activity (personal experience sharing)

Ask students to share their experience about their social support system in their junior middle school study (Who are their social support people and institutions? How much help did they get from them?).

Activity 2: Strong Kids Lesson Review

Use appendix 12.1 to review Strong Kids Lesson.

Activity 3: Enhance an understanding of resilience to school and life success.

Use appendix 12. 2 to improve students' knowledge of resilience to school and life success.

Activity 4: Develop an awareness of social support system.

Use appendix 12. 3 to find out your own social support system.

Activity 5: Skill practice (teamwork) —how to use your social support networks to help you finish your junior middle school study?

Ask students to work in pairs, draw their social support system picture and write down how they can use them to solve their problems and help them to finish their junior middle school study and share it with their partners.

Appendix C: SEL Knowledge Test

On the next few pages, you will be asked to answer questions to see how much you know about feelings, thoughts and behaviors. Read each question carefully and choose what you think is the best answer to each question. You may not know the answers to all the questions and you may not have heard some of the words before, but try your best. You will not be graded on your answers. If you have any questions, please ask your teacher.

True or False

Read each sentence. If you think it is true or mostly true, circle the word "True". If you think it is false or mostly false, circle the word "False".

1. True False Clenched fists and trembling or shaking hands can be signals that tell us to stop and use strategies to solve problems through a situation.
2. True False Emotions feel the same for everyone.
3. True False Stress can be caused by comparing yourself to other people because you think they're doing better than you.
4. True False The way we show how we feel can change depending on who we are with or where we are.
5. True False Feeling uncomfortable is normal and to be expected.
6. True False There are physical feelings or sensations that often happen when we have emotions.

Multiple Choice

Circle the letter that corresponds to the best answer for each question.

7. An example of an emotion that is uncomfortable for most people is "_____

_____".

a. Hopeful

b. Frustrated

c. Curious

d. Excited

8. What is an emotion?

a. A thought you have about a situation.

b. Your inner voice inside your head.

c. A memory you have about something that happened to you.

d. A feeling that tells you something about a situation.

9. Self-talk can be a way to calm down after you get angry. Helpful self-talk might include telling yourself "_____".

a. I don't deserve this

b. I should get angry when something like this happens

c. I can work through it

d. I hope I never see this person ever again

10. Which of the following statements best describes empathy?

a. Knowing how you are feeling.

b. Not knowing why another person is feeling sad.

c. Understanding how another person may be feeling based on your own similar experiences.

d. Wanting another person to feel better soon.

11. Your thoughts can become traps when _____.

a. you see things in a way that is unhelpful or keeps you stuck

b. you see things both the good and bad in each situation

c. you see something different from your friend

d. you think about how another person will feel

12. Reframing is a way to _____.

a. make new friends

b. think about how you can ignore the situation

c. think about a situation differently

d. make sure someone gets in trouble for what he or she has done

13. Why would you want to know how someone else is feeling?

a. So you can leave that person alone when he or she is angry.

b. To better understand and support that person.

c. To tell other people about that person.

d. To act the same when you are together.

14. Conflict resolution is best described as _____.

a. discussing a problem until there is a winner and a loser

b. arguing with another person until he or she sees your point and gives in

c. problem solving so you can reach an agreement that is respectful and responsible for all involved

d. talking about the problems until something changes other person's mind

15. Which of the following is a *positive* or *helpful* way to handle being anxious when you have to show a bad grade to someone like your parent (or guardian)?

a. Tell him or her why you are anxious and that you will work harder next time.

b. Hide your grade and hope he or she will forget about it.

c. Be sad and angry with yourself and stay in your room.

d. Say that your grades were bad because other kids at school distracted you.

16. Which of the following is a helpful way to deal with a problem when you are feeling stressed?

a. Cry somewhere quietly.

b. Talk about the problem with someone you trust, such as a friend or teacher.

c. Throw things around.

d. Ignore the problem.

17. Which of the following is a helpful way to handle your emotions in class when your neighbor's talking begins to annoy you?

a. Yell at that person and tell him or her to stop.

b. Call out to the teacher about the student.

c. Share at the person until he or she knows you're annoyed.

d. Stop and breathe deeply.

18. If you're feeling tired and low in energy, and you're having a hard time enjoying yourself even though things are mostly fine in your life, you could try __

_____.

a. eating healthy meals

b. getting more sleep

c. spending time outdoors

d. spending time with friends

e. any of the above

19. An important step toward achieving goals is knowing how to set them. Which of the following is not an important part of a SMART goal?

a. Specific.

b. Timely.

c. Abstract.

d. Measurable.

20. Your friend seems upset. You want to show your friend that you care about what he or she is feeling. The most helpful way to do this is to _____.

a. talking about something completely different that happened to you to change the subject

b. listen and show that you are paying attention

c. talk about something else

d. look away and don't say anything

Appendix D: Learning Anxiety

Directions: The following 15 questions are about learning anxiety. Please choose the best answer according to your actual situation.

	YES	NO
1. Do you always think about your lessons for tomorrow when you sleep at night?		
2. When the teacher asks questions in class, do you think he or she is asking you to answer the questions, and it makes you feel nervous?	1	0
3. Do you feel nervous when you hear about "exams"?	1	0
4. Are you upset when you don't do well in the exam?	1	0
5. Are you always nervous when your grades are not good?	1	0
6. Do you feel anxious when you can't remember what you learned in class?	1	0
7. Are you always worried after a test until you know your score?	1	0
8. Do you always worry about doing badly in exams?	1	0
9. Do you wish to pass the exam?	1	0
10. Do you always worry about not finishing the task before you finish it?	1	0
11. When you read the text in front of everyone, are you always afraid of making mistakes?	1	0
12. Do you think the school grades are not always reliable?	1	0
13. Do you think you are more worried about learning than others?	1	0
14. Have you ever had a dream that you failed an exam?	1	0
15. Have you ever had a dream of being scolded by your parents or teachers when your grades were poor?	1	0

Appendix E: Dropout Intention

Directions: The following 3 questions are about dropout intention. Please choose the best answer according to your actual situation.

Circumstances	Strongly disagree	Disagree	Slightly disagree	Slightly Agree	agree	Strongly agree
1. I sometimes consider dropping out of school	1	2	3	4	5	6
2. I intend to drop out of school	1	2	3	4	5	6
3. I sometimes feel unsure about continuing my studies year after year	1	2	3	4	5	6

Appendix F: General Causality Orientation Scale (GCOS)

Instruction: These items pertain to a series of hypothetical sketches. Each sketch describes an incident and lists three ways of responding to it. Please read each sketch, imagine yourself in that situation, and then consider each of the possible responses. Think of each response option in terms of the possibility you would respond by that way. (We all respond in a variety of ways to situations, and probably most or all responses are at least slightly likely for you.) If it is very unlikely that you would respond by the way described in a given response, you should circle answer 1 or 2. If it is moderately likely, you would select a number in the midrange, and if it is very likely that you would respond as described, you would circle answer 6.

1.	You have been offered a new position in a company where you have worked for some time. The first question that is likely to come to mind is:	Very unlikely	Unlikely	Slightly unlikely	Slightly likely	Likely	Very likely
(1)	What if I can't live up to the new responsibility?	1	2	3	4	5	6
(2)	Will I do more things at this position?	1	2	3	4	5	6
(3)	I wonder if the new work was interesting.	1	2	3	4	5	6
2.	You have a school-age daughter. On parents' night the teacher tells you that your daughter is doing poorly and doesn't seem involved in the work. You are likely to:	Very unlikely	Unlikely	Slightly unlikely	Slightly likely	Likely	Very likely
(1)	Talk it over with your daughter to further understand the problem	1	2	3	4	5	6
(2)	Scold her and help her do better.	1	2	3	4	5	6
(3)	Make sure she does the assignments, because she should work harder.	1	2	3	4	5	6

Continued table

3.	You had a job interview several weeks ago. In the mail you received a form letter which states that the position has been filled. It is likely that you might think:	Very unlikely	Unlikely	Slightly unlikely	Slightly likely	Likely	Very likely
(1)	It's not what you know, but who you know.	1	2	3	4	5	6
(2)	I'm probably not good enough for the job.	1	2	3	4	5	6
(3)	Somehow they didn't see my qualifications as matching their needs.	1	2	3	4	5	6
4.	You are a plant supervisor and have been charged with the task of allotting coffee breaks to three workers who cannot all break at once. You would likely handle this by:	Very unlikely	Unlikely	Slightly unlikely	Slightly likely	Likely	Very likely
(1)	Telling the three workers the situation and having them work with you on the schedule.	1	2	3	4	5	6
(2)	Simply assigning times that each can break to avoid any problems.	1	2	3	4	5	6
(3)	Find out someone in authority to make sure what to do and what was done in the past.	1	2	3	4	5	6
5.	A close (same-sex) friend of yours has been moody lately, and a couple of times has become very angry with you over "nothing." You might:	Very unlikely	Unlikely	Slightly unlikely	Slightly likely	Likely	Very likely
(1)	Share your observations with him/her and try to find out what is going on for him/her.	1	2	3	4	5	6
(2)	Ignore it because there's not much you can do about it any way.	1	2	3	4	5	6
(3)	Tell him/her that you're willing to spend time together if and only if he/she makes more effort to control him/herself.	1	2	3	4	5	6
6.	You have just received the results of a test you took, and you discovered that you did very poorly. Your initial reaction is likely to be:	Very unlikely	Unlikely	Slightly unlikely	Slightly likely	Likely	Very likely
(1)	"I can't do anything right," and feel sad.	1	2	3	4	5	6
(2)	"I wonder how it is I did so poorly," and feel disappointed.	1	2	3	4	5	6
(3)	"That stupid test doesn't show anything," and feel angry.	1	2	3	4	5	6
7.	You have been invited to a large party where you know very few people. As you look forward to the evening, you would likely expect that:	Very unlikely	Unlikely	Slightly unlikely	Slightly likely	Likely	Very likely
(1)	You'll try to fit in with whatever is happening in order to have a good time and not look bad.	1	2	3	4	5	6
(2)	You'll find some people with whom you can relate.	1	2	3	4	5	6

Continued　table

(3)	You'll probably feel somewhat isolated and unnoticed.	1	2	3	4	5	6
8.	You are asked to plan a picnic for yourself and your fellow employees. Your style for approaching this project could most likely be characterized as:	Very unlikely	Unlikely	Slightly unlikely	Slightly likely	Likely	Very likely
(1)	Take charge: that is, you would make most of the major decisions yourself.	1	2	3	4	5	6
(2)	Follow precedent: you're not really up to the task so you'd do it the way it's been done before.	1	2	3	4	5	6
(3)	Seek participation: get inputs from others who want to make them before you make the final plans.	1	2	3	4	5	6
9.	Recently a position opened up at your place of work that could have meant a promotion for you. However, a person you work with was offered the job rather than you. In evaluating the situation, you're likely to think:	Very unlikely	Unlikely	Slightly unlikely	Slightly likely	Likely	Very likely
(1)	You didn't really expect the job; you frequently get passed over.	1	2	3	4	5	6
(2)	The other person probably "did the right things" politically to get the job.	1	2	3	4	5	6
(3)	You would probably take a look at factors in your own performance that led you to be passed over.	1	2	3	4	5	6
10	You are embarking on a new career. The most important consideration is likely to be:	Very unlikely	Unlikely	Slightly unlikely	Slightly likely	Likely	Very likely
(1)	Whether you can do the work without getting in over your head	1	2	3	4	5	6
(2)	How interested you are in that kind of work.	1	2	3	4	5	6
(3)	Whether there are good possibilities for advancement.	1	2	3	4	5	6
11	A woman who works for you has generally done an adequate job. However, for the past two weeks her work has not been up to par and she appears to be less actively interested in her work. Your reaction is likely to be:	Very unlikely	Unlikely	Slightly unlikely	Slightly likely	Likely	Very likely
(1)	Tell her that her work is below what is expected and that she should start working harder.	1	2	3	4	5	6
(2)	Ask her about the problem and let her know you are available to help work it out.	1	2	3	4	5	6
(3)	It's hard to know what to do to get her straightened out.	1	2	3	4	5	6
12	Your company has promoted you to a position in a city far from your present location. As you think about the move you would probably:	Very unlikely	Unlikely	Slightly unlikely	Slightly likely	Likely	Very likely
(1)	Feel interested in the new challenge and a little nervous at the same time.	1	2	3	4	5	6

(2)	Feel excited about the higher status and salary that is involved.	1	2	3	4	5	6
(3)	Feel stressed and anxious about the upcoming changes.	1	2	3	4	5	6

Appendix G: The Learning Climate Questionnaire (LCQ)

This questionnaire contains items that are related to your experience with your instructor in this class. Instructors have different styles in dealing with students, and we would like to know more about how you have felt about your encounters with your instructor. Your responses are confidential. Please be honest and candid.

	Circumstances	Strongly disagree	Disagree	Slightly disagree	Slightly agree	Agree	Strongly agree
1	I feel that my instructor provides me choices and options.	1	2	3	4	5	6
2	I feel understood by my instructor.	1	2	3	4	5	6
3	My instructor conveys confidence in my ability to do well in the course.	1	2	3	4	5	6
4	My instructor encourages me to ask questions.	1	2	3	4	5	6
5	My instructor listens to how I would like to do things.	1	2	3	4	5	6
6	My instructor tries to understand how I see things before suggesting a new way to do things.	1	2	3	4	5	6

Appendix H: Recruitment Letter

Recruitment Script: Administrator

"Wu Deli, a current Ph. D. student at the Universiti Utara Malaysia in the school of Education and Modern Language, will conduct a research project this Autumn semester, 2019. She is looking for teacher volunteers to participate, along with the students in those classrooms. Participation would include teaching a social and emotional learning based curriculum which intends to help students learn coping skills to deal with everyday life issues. If you are interested in participating, please contact me as soon as possible. Thank you."

Appendix I: Teacher Consent Form

August 2, 2019

Dear Teacher:

Your school has agreed to participate in a research study on a social-emotional learning curriculum conducted by Wu Deli, a doctoral student in the School of Education and Modern Languages, at the Universiti Utara Malaysia, supervised by Professor Dr. Rosna Awang-Hashim and Dr. Kaur Amrita. Resiliency is the capacity to bounce back when presented with life stressors, and a child's possession of resiliency characteristics is related to positive life outcomes.

This study will investigate treatment outcomes when Strong Kids is implemented in self-contained special education classrooms. Outcomes were based on how students respond to a school-based curriculum that teaches skills such as problem-solving, positive thinking, goal-setting, and anger-management. You have been selected as a possible participant in this study because your school provided your name as someone who might be interested in participating in the study. Your district has asked you to participate in a in-service teacher training on Strong Kids. Before beginning implementation of the curriculum, you will be asked on your comfort level in implementation. If you are not yet comfortable in implementation, additional support and training will be provided. Then, class-time was scheduled to deliver the curriculum to all students in your classroom.

The time required to teach the curriculum was approximately 45 minutes per lesson for 12 weeks (1 lesson per week). The Strong Kids lessons will be presented to the students as outlined in the curriculum. Modifications may be made to example situations or scenarios that may be more appropriate for your students. For the purposes of the research, you will be asked to assess students two times, prior to beginning the curriculum and at the end of the 12-week course. The assessment will consist of four questionnaires that the students fill out themselves. The questionnaires ask simple questions about their feelings about themselves, their relationships, and their abilities and would take approximately 15 - 30 minutes to complete in the computer lab.

The scores from these questionnaires will be used to determine the curriculum's impact on students' knowledge of resilience, learning anxiety, and dropout intention. The four assessments include: The SEL knowledge Test, the Learning Anxiety, the Dropout intention and the Learning Climate Questionnaire (LCQ). If you are not already familiar with these measures, you will be provided with training to give these measures. You will be asked to complete one scale by yourself, which is General Causality Orientation Scale (GCOS). We use this scale to check your teaching style. As part of this study, your vice president in your school will also observe you during instruction time of the lessons. The researcher will provide some monetary compensation for your involvement on this project.

To maintain your anonymity, any written information that is obtained in connection with this study will be securely coded and only demographic information, such as gender, years of teaching, and subject area taught was attached to the codes. Participation of districts, schools, teachers, and students is voluntary. Your decision whether or not to participate will not affect your relationship with the Universiti Utara Malaysia, School of Education and Modern Language, your school, or the school district. If you decide to participate, you are free to withdraw your consent and discontinue participation at any time without penalty. Information gathered from this study will not be shared with your school.

If you have any questions, please feel free to contact Wu Deli. Your signature indicates that you have read and understand the information provided above, that you willingly agree to participate, that you may withdraw your consent at any time and discontinue participation without penalty, that you will receive a copy of this form, and that you are not waiving any legal claims, rights or remedies.

Print name and title

_____

School/Grade(s)

_____

Signature and date

_____

Appendix J: Student Consent Form

Dear Student:

I am a Ph. D. student at the Universiti Utara Malaysia. I am interested in helping kids stay strong even when upsetting or difficult things happen in your life. I am doing a project and I would like your help. Your teacher has agreed to help me with my project.

Your teacher is going to teach lessons on how to stay strong. The lessons are called Strong Kids. You will learn about some important skills, like the best thing to do when you feel angry or sad. You will be invited to the computer lab to fill the questionnaires twice. One is before our class, and the other is after our class.

We don't think that the questions will bother you. Some of the questions ask you about your feelings and what you would do at certain times, such as what to do if you are angry. Your teacher will make sure that these examples don't bring up any bad feelings for you. Your teacher will help you to remember that the examples are not real. We can help you with any bad feelings or problems that may come up anytime during completing the packet or in the lessons.

If you decide not to answer the questions, you will not get into any trouble.

If you decide that you want to answer the questions in the packet, just sign your name on the line below. You can change your mind at any time if you no longer want to answer the questions.

Just let the teacher know that you don't want to be a part of the project. You will not get into trouble. Remember that you will answer the questions when you are at school, and there is no grading involved. In fact, all of your answers will be kept a secret so that no one knows whose work it is. We will use a code name instead of your name and the code name will only tell us if you are a girl or a boy, and what class you are in, and what age you are.

If you have any questions about the project, ask your teacher about it, or you can call me.

Sincerely,

Wu Deli

I, _____ , have decided to take part in the packet of questions.

Appendix K: Data Collection and Programs Implementation Schedule

Time	TASSEL intervention	SEL intervention
6th – 8th September, 2019	TASSEL intervention training	SEL intervention training
11th Sept., 2019	Pretest	Pretest
16th – 20th Sept., 2019	Lesson 1 (TASSEL Fidelity Check 1)	Lesson 1 (SEL Fidelity Check 1)
23th – 27th Sept., 2019	Lesson 2	Lesson 2
7th – 11th Oct., 2019	Lesson 3	Lesson 3
14th – 18th Oct., 2019	Lesson 4 (TASSEL Fidelity Check 2)	Lesson 4 (SEL Fidelity Check 2)
21th – 25th Oct., 2019	Lesson 5	Lesson 5
28th – 31th Oct., 2019	Lesson 6	Lesson 6
4th – 8th Nov., 2019	Lesson 7	Lesson 7
11th – 15th Nov., 2019	Lesson 8 (TASSEL Fidelity Check 3)	Lesson 8 (SEL Fidelity Check 3)
18th – 22th Nov., 2019	Lesson 9	Lesson 9
25th – 29th Nov., 2019	Lesson 10	Lesson 10
9th – 13th Dec., 2019	Lesson 11	Lesson 11
16th – 20th Dec., 2019	Lesson 12	Lesson 12
26th Dec., 2019	posttest	posttest

Appendix L: Strong Kids
Intervention Treatment Fidelity

Lesson 1 Fidelity Check 1

<table>
<tr><td colspan="5" align="center">Lesson 1</td></tr>
<tr><td>Start time:</td><td colspan="4">End time:</td></tr>
<tr><td rowspan="2">Lesson component</td><td colspan="3" align="center">Level of implication</td><td rowspan="2">Notes</td></tr>
<tr><td>Not</td><td>Partial</td><td>Full</td></tr>
<tr><td>Introduction</td><td>☐</td><td>☐</td><td>☐</td><td></td></tr>
<tr><td>Focusing activity</td><td>☐</td><td>☐</td><td>☐</td><td></td></tr>
<tr><td>Lesson topics</td><td>☐</td><td>☐</td><td>☐</td><td></td></tr>
<tr><td>Key terms</td><td>☐</td><td>☐</td><td>☐</td><td></td></tr>
<tr><td>Activity A</td><td>☐</td><td>☐</td><td>☐</td><td></td></tr>
<tr><td>Activity B</td><td>☐</td><td>☐</td><td>☐</td><td></td></tr>
<tr><td>Putting It all together</td><td></td><td></td><td></td><td></td></tr>
<tr><td>Closure</td><td>☐</td><td>☐</td><td>☐</td><td></td></tr>
<tr><td colspan="5">Lesson notes:</td></tr>
</table>

Lesson 4 Fidelity Check 2

Lesson 4			
Start time:		End time:	
Review	Level of implication		Notes
	Not　　Partial　　Full		
Introduction	☐　　☐　　☐		
Focusing activity	☐　　☐　　☐		
Key terms	☐　　☐　　☐		
Activity A	☐　　☐　　☐		
Activity B	☐　　☐　　☐		
Activity C	☐　　☐　　☐		
Activity D	☐　　☐　　☐		
Putting It all together	☐　　☐　　☐		
Closure	☐　　☐　　☐		
Lesson notes:			

Lesson 8 Fidelity Check 3

Lesson 8			
Start time:		End time:	
Review	Level of implication		Notes
	Not　　Partial　　Full		
Introduction	☐　　☐　　☐		

Continued   table

Lesson 8			
Start time:		End time:	
Focusing activity	☐	☐	☐
Key terms	☐	☐	☐
Activity A	☐	☐	☐
Activity B	☐	☐	☐
Activity C	☐	☐	☐
Activity D	☐	☐	☐
Putting It all together	☐	☐	☐
Closure	☐	☐	☐
Lesson notes:			

Appendix M: Teacher Autonomy Supportive Strong Kids Intervention Treatment Fidelity

Lesson 1 TASSEL Fidelity Check 1

Lesson 1				
Start time: End time:				
Teacher autonomy supportive behavior in each session	Level of implication			Notes
	Not	Partial	Full	
I. Start session Allow students to choose their seats and sit with their friends	☐	☐	☐	
II. Structure session Give structure about each lesson	☐	☐	☐	
III. Ration alize session Provide rationale for activities linked to the lesson	☐	☐	☐	
IV. Teaching activities	☐	☐	☐	
1. Ask students to share their own experiments and accept students' negative emotions	☐	☐	☐	
2. Ask students to draw or write about their feelings	☐	☐	☐	
3. Allow group discussion with teamwork	☐	☐	☐	
Lesson notes:				

Lesson 4 TASSEL Fidelity Check 2

<table>
<tr><td colspan="5" align="center">Lesson 4
Start time: End time:</td></tr>
<tr><td rowspan="2">Teacher autonomy supportive behavior in each session</td><td colspan="3" align="center">Level of implication</td><td rowspan="2">Notes</td></tr>
<tr><td>Not</td><td>Partial</td><td>Full</td></tr>
<tr><td>I. Start session
Allow students to choose their seats and sit with their friends</td><td>☐</td><td>☐</td><td>☐</td><td></td></tr>
<tr><td>II. Structure session
Give structure about each lesson</td><td>☐</td><td>☐</td><td>☐</td><td></td></tr>
<tr><td>III. Ration session
Give rational on activities according to the lesson</td><td>☐</td><td>☐</td><td>☐</td><td></td></tr>
<tr><td>IV. Teaching activities</td><td></td><td></td><td></td><td></td></tr>
<tr><td>1. Ask students to share their own experiments and accept students' negative emotions</td><td>☐</td><td>☐</td><td>☐</td><td></td></tr>
<tr><td>2. Ask students to draw or write about their feelings</td><td>☐</td><td>☐</td><td>☐</td><td></td></tr>
<tr><td>3. Allow group discussion with teamwork</td><td>☐</td><td>☐</td><td>☐</td><td></td></tr>
<tr><td colspan="5">Lesson notes:</td></tr>
</table>

Lesson 8 TASSEL Fidelity Check 3

Lesson 8				
Start time:		End time:		
Teacher autonomy supportive behavior in each session	Level of implication			Notes
	Not	Partial	Full	
I. Start session Allow students to choose their seats and sit with their friends	□	□	□	
II. Structure session Give structure about each lesson	□	□	□	
III. Ration session Give rational on activities according to the lesson	□	□	□	
IV. Teaching activities	□	□	□	
1. Ask students to share their own experiments and accept students' negative emotions	□	□	□	
2. Ask students to draw or write about their feelings	□	□	□	
3. Allow group discussion with teamwork	□	□	□	
Lesson notes:				

Appendix N: Sample
Pacing Communication

Dear Teachers,

Thank you to all of you for your diligent efforts with both the lessons and the fidelity checklists. I am hearing great things about how the kids are talking about the Strong Kids lessons. It really warms my heart to hear about them making great choices even if it is for a little pooch! Love to hear about your success and/or challenges. It makes us all better as we grow our kids together.

If you are missing any assessment, I put them in your boxes along with next week's fidelity checklist.

Remember to put all fidelity checklists in my box, bring them to me directly, or send me an email and I will come to get it!

As always, if there is anything I can do to ease the implementation process, let me know. Thank you for always doing what's the best for our kids.

REFERENCES

Abramson, L. Y., Seligman, M. E., & Teasdale, J. D. (1978). Learned helplessness in humans: critique and reformulation. *Journal of abnormal psychology*, 1987(1), 49.

Adams, & David Wallace, (1995). Education for extinction: American Indians and the boarding school experience, 1875 – 1928. History: *Reviews of New Books.* 24 (4), 154 – 155.

Adetunji, A., & Oladeji, B. O. (2007). Comparative study of the reading habit of boarding and day secondary school students in Osogbo, Osun State, Nigeria. *Pakistan Journal of Social Science*, 4(4), 509 – 512.

Ary, D., Jacobs, L. C., & Razavieh, A. (1972). *Introduction to research in education*. Holt, Rinehart & Winston.

Baer, D. M., Wolf, M. M., & Risley, T. R. (1987). Some still-current dimensions of applied behavior analysis. *Journal of Applied Behavior Analysis*, 20 (4), 313 – 327.

Barch, J. (2006). *From teachers' autonomy supportiveness training to students' intrinsic motivation*. Paper presented at the Annual Meeting of the American Psychological Association, New Orleans, LA, August.

Barrios, B. A., & Hartmann, D. P. (1997). Fears and anxieties. In E. J. Mash & L. G. *Terdal (Eds.), Assessment of childhood disorders* (3rd ed., pp. 230 – 327). New York: Guilford Press.

Barlas, N. S., Sidhu, J., & Li, C. (2021). Can social-emotional learning programs be adapted to schools in Pakistan? A literature review. *International journal of school & educational psychology*, 1 – 15.

Benner, G. , Kutash, K. , Nelson, J. , & Fisher, M. (2013). Closing the achievement gap of youth with emotional and behavioral disorders through multi-tiered systems of support. *Education and treatment of children*, 36 (3), 15 – 29.

Bichao, H. (2005). An analysis of the poverty of culture that causes junior middle school students to drop out of school in Guangxi Frontier Region. *Journal of Nanning junior teachers' college*.

Boyes, M. E. , Berg, V. , & Cluver, L. D. (2017). Poverty moderates the association between gender and school dropout in South African adolescents. *Vulnerable children and youth studies*, 12 (3), 195 – 206.

Brislin, R. W. (1970). Back-translation for cross-cultural research. *Journal of cross-cultural psychology*, 1 (3), 185 – 216.

Brown, P. H. , & Park, A. (2002). Education and poverty in rural China. *Economics of education review*, 21 (6), 523 – 541.

Bruni, L. (2015). *The impact of teaching of social emotional skills on student and teacher perception of school success* (Doctoral dissertation), University of St. Francis, Francis, USA.

Carrizales-Engelmann, D. , Merrell, K. W. , Feuerborn, L. , Gueldner, B. A. , & Tran, O. K. (2016). *Merrell's strong teens, grades 9 – 12: A social and emotional learning curriculum*. Brookes Publishing.

Carta, J. J. (2002). An early childhood special education research agenda in a culture of accountability for results. *Journal of early intervention*, 25, 102 – 104.

Castro-Olivo, S. M. (2014). Promoting social-emotional learning in adolescent Latino ELLs: A study of the culturally adapted strong teens program. *School psychology quarterly*, 29 (4), 567 – 577.

Chang, C. L. H. , & Chen, J. Q. (2017). The information ethics perception gaps between Chinese and American students. *Information technology & people*.

Chatzisarantis, N. L. , & Hagger, M. S. (2009). Effects of an intervention based on self-determination theory on self-reported leisure-time physical activity participation. *Psychology and health*, 24, 29 – 48.

Cheon, S. H. , & Reeve, J. (2015). A classroom-based intervention to help teachers decrease students' amotivation. *Contemporary educational psychology*, 40, 99 – 111.

Collins, R. (2001). *Teachers' motivating styles and educational change*. Dissertation abstracts international, 61 (9 – A), 3463.

Condly, S. J. (2006). Resilience in children: A review of literature with implications for education. *Urban education*, 41 (3), 211 – 236.

Connelly, R. , & Zheng, Z. (2003). Determinants of school enrolment and completion of 10 to 18 years old in China. *Economics of education review*, 22 (4), 379 – 388.

Conoley, J. C. , & Gutkin, T. B. (2017). School psychology: A reconceptualization of service delivery realities. In the delivery of psychological services in schools (pp. 393 – 424).

Cookson, P. W. (2009). *"Boarding schools," in R. A. Shweder (Ed.)*, *The child: An encyclopedic companion*. Chicago: University of Chicago Press, 112 – 114.

Cowen, E. (1994). The enhancement of psychological wellness: Challenges and opportunities. *American journal of community psychology*, 22 (2), 149 – 79.

Creswell, J. W. (2012). *Educational research: planning, conducting, and evaluating quantitative and qualitative research* (4th ed.). Pearson Education.

Culp, R. (2020). Articulating citizenship: Civic education and student politics in Southeastern China, 1912 – 1940. Brill. *Articulating citizenship*. Harvard University Asia Center

Dawson, C. (2007). *A practical guide to research methods*. A user-friendly manual for mastering research techniques and projects (3rd ed.). United Kingdom: How to Books, Oxford.

Deci, E. L. , & Ryan, R. M. (1985). *Intrinsic motivation and self-determination in human behavior*. New York: Plenum.

Deci, E. L. , & Ryan, R. M. (1987). The support of autonomy and the control of behavior. *Journal of personality and social psychology*, 53, 1024 – 1037.

Deci, E. L. , & Ryan, R. M. (2002). *Overview of self-determination theory: An organismic dialectical perspective.* Handbook of self-determination research, 3 – 33.

Deci, E. L. , & Ryan, R. M. (2008). Self-determination theory: A macro theory of human motivation, development, and health. *Canadian psychology*, 49 (3), 182.

Denham, S. A. , & Brown, C. (2010). Plays nice with others: Social-emotional learning and academic success. *Early education and development*, 21 (5), 652 – 680.

Dimitrov, D. M. , & Rumrill Jr, P. D. (2003). Pretest-posttest designs and measurement of change. *Work*, 20 (2), 159 – 165.

Durlak, J. A. , Weissberg, R. P. , Dymnicki, A. B. , Taylor, R. D. , & Schellinger, K. B. (2011). The impact of enhancing students' social and emotional learning: A meta-analysis of school-based universal interventions. *Child development*, 82 (1), 405 – 432.

Edmonds, W. A. , & Kennedy, T. D. (2016). *An applied guide to research designs: Quantitative, qualitative, and mixed methods.* Sage Publications.

Edmunds, J. , Ntoumanis, N. , & Duda, J. L. (2008). Testing a self-determination theory based teaching style intervention in the exercise domain. *European journal of social psychology*, 38 (2), 375 – 388.

Eicher, V. , Staerklé, C. , & Clémence, A. (2014). I want to quit education: A longitudinal study of stress and optimism as predictors of school dropout intention. *Journal of adolescence*, 37 (7), 1021 – 1030.

Faust, J. J. (2006). *Preventing depression and anxiety: An evaluation of a social-emotional curriculum.* (Unpublished education specialist's thesis), University of Wisconsin, USA.

Filmer, D. (1999). The structure of social disparities in education: Gender and wealth. Policy research report on gender and development. Working paper series, No. 5.

Freudenberg, N., & Ruglis, J. (2007). Peer reviewed: Reframing school dropout as a public health issue. *Preventing chronic disease*, 4 (4).

Gardner, H. (1983). *Frame of mind: The theory of multiple intelligence*. New York, NY: Basic Books.

Glewwe, P., & Kremer, M. (2006). Schools, teachers, and education outcomes in developing countries. *Handbook of the economics of education*, 2, 945 – 1017.

Goleman, D. (1995). *Emotional intelligence*. New York: Bantam Books, Inc.

Goleman, D. (2000). Leadership that gets results. *Harvard business review*, 78 (2), 4 – 17.

Goodwin, C. J. (2010). *Research in psychology methods and design* (6th ed.). United States: John Wiley & Sons.

Gravetter, F. J., & Forzano, L. (2012). *Research methods for the behavioral sciences* (4th ed.). Belmont, CA: Wadsworth.

Guay, F., Ratelle, C. F., & Chanal, J. (2008). Optimal learning in optimal contexts: The role of self-determination in education. *Canadian psychology*, 49 (3), 233 – 240.

Gueldner, B. A. & Feuerborn, L. L. (2016). Bridging mindfulness-based practices with social and emotional learning: A conceptual review and application. *Mindfulness*, 7, 164 – 175.

Gunter, L., Caldarella, P., Korth, B. B., & Young, K. R. (2012). Promoting social and emotional learning in preschool students: A study of strong start Pre-K. *Early childhood education journal*, 40 (3), 151 – 159.

Halle, J. (1998). Fidelity: A crucial question in translating research to practice. *Journal of early intervention*, 21, 294 – 296.

Hambleton, R. K., Merenda, P. F., & Spielberger, C. D. (2004). *Adapting educational and psychological tests for cross-cultural assessment*. London: LEA.

Hardré, P. L., & Reeve, J. (2009). Benefits of training corporate managers to adopt a more autonomy supportive style toward employees: an intervention study. *International journal of training and development*, 13 (3), 165 – 184.

Harlacher, J. E. , & Merrell, K. W. (2010). Social and emotional learning as a universal level of student support: Evaluating the follow-up effect of Strongkids on social and emotional outcomes. *Journal of Applied School Psychology*, 26 (3), 212 – 229.

Horner, R. , & Sugai, G. (2015). School-wide PBIS: An example of applied behavior analysis implemented at a scale of social importance. *Behavior analysis in practice*, 8 (1), 80 – 85.

Howard, B. (2014). *An examination of the effects of the Strong start pre-kindergarten program on the behaviors of children with externalizing behavior disorders in a therapeutic preschool*. The University of Utah.

Ingham, J. C. , & Riley, G. (1998). Guidelines for documentation of treatment efficacy for young children who stutter. *Journal of Speech, Language, and Hearing Research*, 41 (4), 753 – 770.

Jang, H. , Reeve, J. , & Deci, E. L. (2010). Engaging students in learning activities: It is not autonomy support or structure but autonomy support and structure. *Journal of educational psychology*, 102 (3), 588.

Keppel, G. & Wickens, T. D. (2004) Design and Analysis: *A Researcher's Handbook*, 4th edn, Prentice Hall, Upper Saddle River, NJ.

Kirk, D. (1995). 'Thanks for the history lesson': Some thoughts on a pedagogical use of history in educational research and practice. *The Australian Educational Researcher*, 22 (3), 1 – 20.

Kramer, T. J. (2013). Evaluating social and emotional learning curriculum, Strong Kids, implemented school-wide (*Doctoral dissertation*).

Leech, N. , Barrett, K. , & Morgan, G. A. (2013). *SPSS for intermediate statistics: Use and interpretation*. Routledge.

Li, F. (2017). *Investigation on mental health problems of rural junior middle school students in remote mountainous areas and research on coping mechanisms*. Doctor's degree thesis of Jilin University.

Li, F. Z. , Yang, C. L. , & Huang, M. (2018). Course orientation of social emotional learning in China. *Guangxi education*, (12), 40 −45.

Li, Q. , Zang, W. , & An, L. (2013). Peer effects and school dropout in rural China. *China economic review*, 27, 238 −248.

Liu, C. , Zhang, L. , Luo, R. , Rozelle, S. , Sharbono, B. , & Shi, Y. (2009). Development challenges, tuition barriers, and high school education in China. *Asia pacific journal of education*, 29, 503 −520.

Lu, M. , (2009), Reasons of implementing the nutrition project in rural boarding schools and its effectiveness, *China development research foundation report No. 51* [In Chinese].

Marshall, J. H. , Aguilar, C. R. , Alas, M. , Castellanos, R. R. , Castro, L. , Enamorado, R. , & Fonseca, E. (2014). Alternative education programmes and middle school dropout in Honduras. *International Review of Education*, 60, 51 −77.

Mayer, J. D. , & Salovey, P. (1995). Emotional intelligence and the construction and regulation of feelings. *Applied and preventive psychology*, 4 (3), 197 −208.

Mayer, J. , & Salovey, P. (1990). Emotional intelligence. *Imagination, cognition, and personality*. Psychological inquiry, 9 (3), 185 −211.

McDonald, A. S. (2001). *The prevalence and effects of test anxiety in school children.* Educational psychology, 21, 89 −101.

McKown, C. (2017). Social-emotional assessment, performance, and standards. *The future of children*, 157 −178.

McLeod, J. D. , & Kaiser, K. (2004). Childhood emotional and behavioral problems and educational attainment. *American sociological review*, 69, 636 −658.

Merrell, K. W. (2010). Linking prevention science and social and emotional learning: The oregon resiliency project. *Psychology in the schools*, 47 (1), 55 −70.

Merrell, K. W. , Carrizales, D. C. , Feuerborn, L. C. , Gueldner, B. A. , & Tran, O. K. (2007). *Strong Kids Grades 6 − 8: A social and emotional learning curriculum.* Paul H Brookes Publishing.

Merrell, K. W. , Juskelis, M. P. , Tran, O. K. , & Buchanan, R. (2008). Social and emotional learning in the classroom: Evaluation of Strongkids and Strong Teens on students' social-emotional knowledge and symptoms. *Journal of Applied School Psychology*, 24 (2), 209 – 224.

Merrell, K. W. (2011). Social and emotional assets and resilience scales (SEARS). Lutz, FL: Psychological assessment resources.

Moretti, J. (2010). Screening with no smoke or mirrors. RtI Network. Retrieved from *www. rtinetwork. org/rti-blog/entry/*1/96.

Moswela, B. , (2006). Boarding schools as perpetrators of students' behavior problems. *Journal of social science*,13 (1), 37 – 41.

Murfin, G. D. and N. L. Jamieson, (1977). Boarding schools: Effects on the psychological health of Eskimo adolescents. *American journal of psychiatry*, 134 (4), 411.

National Bureau of Statistics, (2016). China statistical yearbook, *Beijing: China Statistics Press.*

Pang, Lijuan and Xiaoyu Han, (2005). The structural adjustment of primary schools and junior high schools in rural China: Problems, reasons and solutions. *Journal of Educational Studies*, 1 (8), 90 – 96 [In Chinese].

Papworth, B. A. , (2014). *Attending boarding school: A longitudinal study of its role in students' academic and non-academic outcomes.* Doctoral dissertation, University of Sydney, Australia.

Petrides, K. V. , Pita, R. , & Kokkinaki, F. (2007). The location of trait emotional intelligence in personality factor space. *British journal of psychology*, 98, 273 – 281.

Plumb, J. L. , Bush, K. A. , & Kersevich, S. E. (2016). Trauma-sensitive schools: An evidence-based approach. *School social work journal*, 40 (2). 37 – 60.

Qiao, L. , Chen, X. N. , Yuan, P. , Su, W. , Zeng, J. , (2008). Status of mental health of the left-behind children in certain regions of Sichuan. *Modern preventive medicine.* 35 (16) (Chinese).

Qinzhou Municipal People's Government (2019), Retrieved from *http: //www. qinzhou. gov. cn/glqz_ 205/rk/.*

Reddy, A. N. , & Sinha, S. (2010). *School dropouts or pushouts? Overcoming barriers for the right to education.* Consortium for research on educational access, transitions and equity monograph No. 40.

Reeve, J. (1998). Autonomy support as an interpersonal motivating style: Is it teachable? *Contemporary educational psychology*, 23 (3), 312 – 330.

Reeve, J. , & Halusic, M. (2009). How K-12 teachers can put self-determination theory principles into practice. *Theory and research in education*, 7, 145 – 154.

Reeve, J. , & Jang, H. (2006). What teachers say and do to support students' autonomy during a learning activity. *Journal of educational psychology*, 98 (1), 209.

Reeve, J. , Jang, H. , Carrell, D. , Barch, J. , & Jeon, S. (2004). Enhancing high school students' engagement by increasing their teachers' autonomy support. *Motivation and emotion*, 28 (2), 147 – 169.

Reio Jr, T. G. , & Shuck, B. (2015). Exploratory factor analysis: implications for theory, research, and practice. A*dvances in developing human resources*, 17 (1), 12 – 25.

Reynolds, C. R. , & Richmond, B. O. (1978). What I think and feel: A revised measure of children's manifest anxiety. *Journal of abnormal child psychology*, 6 (2), 271 – 280.

Romer, N. , & Merrell, K. W. (2013). Temporal stability of strength-based assessments: Test-retest reliability of student and teacher reports. *Assessment for effective intervention*, 38, 185 – 191.

Schonert-Reichl, K. , Roeser, R. W. , & Maloney, J. E. (2016). *Handbook of mindfulness in education: integrating theory and research into practice.* New York: Springer.

Shaughnessy, J. J. , Zechmeister, E. B. , & Zechmeister, J. S. (2012). *Research methods in psychology* (9th ed.). New York: McGraw-Hill

Companies.

Shi, Y. , Zhang, L. , Ma, Y. , Yi, H. , Liu, C. , Johnson, N. , Chu, J. , Loyalka, P. & Rozelle, S. (2015). Dropping out of rural china's secondary schools: A mixed-methods analysis. *China Quarterly*, 224, 1048 – 1069.

Shu, Binbin and Yuying Tong, (2015). *Boarding at school and students' well-being: The case of rural china.* Population Association of America 2015 Annual Meeting.

Spielberger, C. D. , & Vagg, P. R. (1995). *Test anxiety: Theory, assessment, and treatment.* Washington, DC: Taylor & Francis.

Su, Y. L. , & Reeve, J. (2011). A meta-analysis of the effectiveness of intervention programs designed to support autonomy. *Educational psychology review*, 23, 159 – 188.

Sullivan, G. S. (2005). The effects of a coaching education workshop on the self-regulated motivation of 6th Grade male and female basketball players. *Dissertation abstracts international*, 66 (5 – B), 2850.

Tereza & Slivinska, (2018). *Analysis and trial study on the textbooks of "Strong Kids" in Grade 6 – 8 in the United States.* Master's degree thesis of Shanghai Normal University.

Thorndike, E. (1920). Intelligence and its uses. *Harper's Magazine*, 140, 227 – 235.

Turnbull, H. R. , & Turnbull, A. P. (2000). Accountability: Who's job is it anyway? *Journal of early intervention*, 23, 231 – 234.

U. S. Department of Education. (2017). *The Elementary and Secondary Education Act of* 1965, as amended by the Every Student Succeeds Act.

United Nations Educational, Scientific, & Cultural Organization (UNESCO). (2012). *Opportunities lost: The impact of Grade repetition and early school leaving.* Institute of Statistics Global Education Digest.

Wang, Ting & Wen Li, (2009). The nutrition of primary boarding students in poor rural China and its determinants. *Journal of Ningxia Teachers University*,

Vol. 30, No. 2, pp. 118 – 122 [In Chinese].

Whitcomb, S., & Parisi Damico, D. M. (2016). *Merrell's strong start*, *grades K-2: A social and emotional learning curriculum* (2nd ed.). Baltimore, MD: Brookes Publishing.

White, N. J., & Rayle, A. D. (2007). Strong Teens: A school-based small group experience for African American males. *The journal for specialists in group work*, 32 (2), 178 – 189.

Williams, G. C., Cox, E. M., Kouides, R., & Deci, E. L. (1999). Presenting the facts about smoking to adolescents: The effects of an autonomy supportive style. *Archives of pediatrics and adolescent medicine*, 153, 959 – 964.

Williams, G. C., Gagné, M., Ryan, R. M., & Deci, E. L. (2002). Facilitating autonomous motivation for smoking cessation. *Health psychology*, 21, 40 – 50.

Williams, G. C., Wiener, M. W., Markakis, K. M., Reeve, J., & Deci, E. L. (1994). Medical students' motivation for internal medicine. *Journal of general internal medicine*, 9 (6), 327 – 333.

Wu, Z. H. (2016). *Report on the development of rural education in China* 2016, Beijing: Beijing Normal University Press.

Yao, Y., Kang, Y., Gong, W., Chen, Y., & Zhang, L. (2011). MHT scale of adolescent with different gender: A meta-analysis. *Chinese journal of evidence-based medicine*, 11, 211 – 219.

Yue, Ai, Yao jiang Shi, & Fang Chang et al., (2014). Dormitory management and boarding students in China's rural primary schools. *China agricultural economic review*, 6 (3), 523 – 550.

Zai, Yue & Ying Xuan, (2011). Analysis on problems among life teachers in rural boarding schools. *Theory learning*, 7, 217 – 219 [In Chinese].

Zhao, Y. J., & Lu, Y. (2020). Mapping determinants of rural poverty in Guangxi—a less developed region of China. *Journal of Mountain Science*, 17 (7), 1749 – 1762.

Zhang, G. Y., (2006). A survey on mental health of rural middle-school students. *Studies of psychology and behavior.* 4 (3), 180 – 183 (Chinese).

Zhou, B. (1991). *Mental health test (MHT).* Shanghai: East China Normal University Press.

Zhu, Xiaoming, Jiahu Hao, & Yexun Liu, (2008). Smoking and drinking behavior among rural boarding school students in Anhui Province. *Chinese journal of school health*, 29 (9), 791 – 793 [In Chinese].

Zhu, H., & Hou, L. (2020). Let education play a more role in rural revitalization—Taking Guangxi border ethnic areas as an example. *Journal of contemporary educational research*, 4 (6).

List of Abbreviations

MoE	Ministry of Education
HSEE	High School Entrance Examination
MTSS	Multi-tiered Systems of Support
CASEL	Collaborative for Academic, Social and Emotional Learning
SEL	Social and Emotional Learning
PT	Psychology Teacher
RT	Regular Teacher
TAS	Teacher Autonomy Support
TASSEL	Teacher Autonomy Supportive Social and Emotional Learning
ASIP	Autonomy Support Intervention Program
LCQ	Learning Climate Questionnaire
GCOS	General Causality Orientation Scale